Mary McCarthy

HANOI

HARCOURT, BRACE & WORLD, INC., NEW YORK

To Daniel, Alison, and Jonathan
and their father,
Captain, U.S. Air Force,
World War II

Contents

Foreword

As a preparatory exercise, the reader may be interested in the following controversy, which took place in The New York Review of Books *a few months before my visit to Hanoi. The occasion was the magazine publication of "Solutions." Early in 1967, I had visited South Vietnam, and the result was a short book,* Vietnam. *"Solutions," its final chapter, disclaimed the ability to prescribe how the United States should get out of Vietnam. It was up to Johnson and his advisers, I said, to find the way out. They put the troops there; let them extricate them. My job as an intellectual was to insist as intractably as I knew how on stopping the war, not to offer face-saving formulas for doing so. If Johnson wanted to get out of Vietnam, he could, and this, by the way, has been true all along and remains true this minute. For example, today, this morning, he could stop the bombing of the North.*

The obstacles in the way of a U.S. retreat are largely imaginary, in the sense that they would yield before a real sense of urgency. They are the classic obstacles that confront any commander or chief of state who is obliged, for moral or other reasons, to pull out of an untenable position, that confronted Churchill at Dunkirk and De Gaulle in Algeria: how to minimize the loss of your own men and matériel and what will happen to your allies when you leave. Mrs. Trilling thinks that the second consideration ought to have weighed heavier on my conscience, instead of figuring in a mere parenthesis "(and what about the 'loyal' Vietnamese—should they be left behind or do we owe them an airlift to Taiwan?)." Her letter, I felt, required reply in that it stated the arguments usually advanced for our staying in Vietnam. The fact that Mrs. Trilling, as the reader will see, does not *advocate our staying in Vietnam reduces those arguments to the state of mere scruples or perplexities. Yet I am grateful to her for prompting me to deal with them and for her permission to reprint her letter.*

M. McC.

On Withdrawing from Vietnam:
An Exchange

Diana Trilling:

Mary McCarthy's proposal in her recent article, "Vietnam: Solutions" (November 9), that we should stop worrying about means of terminating the war and concentrate our full energies on simply getting it brought to an end, is bound to be warmly welcomed by many opponents of the war. This is a weary time. It cannot but be a relief to be told that political effort, as it is demonstrated by the error and insufficiency of the present Administration both in foreign and domestic affairs, is unworthy of the intellectual life as that life is defined by its commitment to morality.

But unfortunately, in clearing the decks for an acceleration of protest unimpeded by practical political concerns, Miss McCarthy leaves one consideration out of account. She fails to mention, except in a contemptuous reference to airlifting "loyal" Vietnamese (the quotation marks are hers) to Taiwan, the problem which for some opponents of the war, myself included, makes the central issue of the Vietnam situation— what happens after America withdraws. Reading Miss McCarthy's piece one might suppose that "solution" of the war is just a matter of saving face for Johnson by finding a suitable device for negotiation of peace, and of evacuating half a million troops.

These problems Miss McCarthy assigns to the professional politicians and military tacticians—and who would not agree with her? A division of labor which spares intellectuals for thought, and leaves strategies and logistics to those who are trained in them, is eminently sensible. But the fact is that the question of how we should or should not go about negotiation of a peace settlement is not, as Miss McCarthy would have us think, "merely" political. It is a political problem which is also nothing if not a moral problem: it involves the fate of millions of human beings, at least as many as are involved by our presence in Vietnam. If South Vietnam falls to the Communists, who stifle opposition and kill their enemies, is this not of moral concern to intellectuals? Or is the disfavor in which we hold our present practice of democracy a sufficient warrant to regard Communism as the party of peace and freedom? Certainly Miss McCarthy's refusal to deal with a Communist victory in South Vietnam as any kind of threat to the values she would wish to see multiplied in the world characterizes the preference of American intellectuals for addressing but a single moral culprit, America. But this is a game we play. Most of us know better.

Miss McCarthy cites Kennan, Fulbright, Galbraith, Schlesinger, and Goodwin as instances of the way in which concern with political "solutions" can lead intellectuals to the betrayal of their sole moral duty, protest of the war. In these unhappy examples she would have us recognize an inevitable connection between engagement with the practical aspects of politics and a deteriorated moral sentiment—seemingly, when these men undertook to offer positive suggestions for how this country might proceed to end the war they were in objective effect conspiring with a government they were morally obligated to oppose and only oppose. Surely this carries us rather far in disgust with politics—if moral man is permitted only a negative relation to government, one wonders what keeps all of us who think of ourselves as moral persons from declaring ourselves Anarchists.

One also wonders whether Miss McCarthy, jealous as she is for the special domain of intellectuals, has let herself realize that by limiting the political role of intellectuals wholly to that of dissent she deprives them of an historical privilege they have claimed with some authority—the right to propose and even direct the positive operations of government. It is an honorable roster she now closes to us and it includes—need one remind her—not only liberals content to work within the given structure of the State but also radicals and even revolutionaries who wanted, and sometimes succeeded in achieving, actual governing power.

That old vexed question of the responsibility of intellectuals is, I know, not to be settled in debate with Miss McCarthy. And I am aware that the position she has taken in her article, that the single job of intellectuals and indeed of all decent people is to get us out of Vietnam, the sooner the better and who cares by what means or what follows on our withdrawal, is far too emotionally attractive to yield before a contrary view—namely, that no choice which is careless of its consequences is a moral choice. I think America was and is careless of certain deeply important consequences of going into Vietnam. I hardly think this justifies intellectuals in being similarly careless of the consequences of our getting out.

I too oppose this war and urge our withdrawal from Vietnam, on the well-explored ground that America cannot militarily win the third world from Communism without the gravest danger of thermonuclear war or, at the least, without conduct inconsistent with and damaging to the democratic principle and the principle of national sovereignty we would hope to protect and extend— the fact that in order to be even as little successful as we have so far been in resisting the Viet Cong America has in effect possessed the sovereign territory of South Vietnam dramatizes the threat to the autonomy of small nations inherent in such ill-considered procedures. But even as I take this stand I confront the grim reality that in withdrawing from Vietnam we consign untold numbers of Southeast Asian opponents of Communism to their death and countless more to the abrogation of the right of protest which we American intellectuals hold so dear. And if, unhappily, I have no answer to the torturing question of what can be done to save these distant lives, I don't regard this as proof of my moral purity or as an escape from what Miss McCarthy calls the "booby-trap" of "solutions." I hope that everyone, including intellectuals, will keep on trying to find the answer I lack. For without this effort the moral intransigence for which Miss McCarthy speaks is its own kind of callousness.

Mary McCarthy:

Mrs. Trilling has the gift of prophecy. I have not. I do not know what will happen to millions of human beings in Southeast Asia if the Americans pull out. Common sense suggests that the richer and more visible of the "loyal" South Vietnamese will follow their bank accounts to France and Switzerland. Quotation marks are called for since what these people are loyal to has not been determined. Their duly constituted government? Their country? Democratic principle? Their skins? When the Americans use the word, they mean loyal to *them*: "We can't let these guys down because they have stuck with us." Yet the depth of this sense of togetherness can be gauged by what happened to Diem, an outstanding "good Indian" who became a liability.

Let us drop the crocodile concern and talk about realities. It is perfectly true that many thousands of South Vietnamese have been compromised by working for the Americans, as interpreters, language teachers, nurses, drivers, construction workers, cleaning women, cooks, PX employees, and so on; there are at least 140,000 on the military payroll alone. No outsider can be long in Vietnam without feeling some misgivings as to what may happen to them "afterward." Their employers must occasionally ponder this, too. One can hope that an AID official, hurriedly packing to leave, will feel some qualms about Minh, who has been driving his car, that a few Marines will think twice about Kim, the girl who works in the canteen. But this is not politics but ordinary ethics: a responsibility felt for people whose lives have touched one's own and who therefore cannot be expected to vanish like stage scenery when the action shifts elsewhere.

In exceptional cases, something *will* be done, on a person-to-person basis, assuming Minh's and Kim's willingness: jobs and "sponsorship" will be found in the U.S.; voluntary agencies on the spot will help; neutral embassies will help. But the majority will be left to face the music; that is the tough luck of being a camp follower. The departure of an occupying force, the closing-down of an embassy or a mission means the curt abandonment of the local employees to the mercies of fortune and their compatriots. It happened in France last spring when the U.S. NATO forces were ordered out: what became of the 17,500 "faithful" French employees? It can be argued that that is De Gaulle's worry.

The work force of South Vietnamese who have "cast in their lot" with the Americans has drifted into politics through the accident or fatality of economics: they were looking for a job. Nobody could seriously place them among the "untold numbers of opponents of Communism," though in a literal sense that is what they are, and it is they, no doubt, who will have risked the most in the end if the sanguinary scenes imagined by Mrs. Trilling actually are enacted. In that event, one can hope for their sakes that they were secretly working for the Viet Cong (a suspicion that falls on them anyway), in short that they were political after all.

RVN government figures, who have contributed far less to the war effort, in fact who have positively hampered it through graft and other forms of crookedness, are more likely to benefit from a grateful U.S. The Seventh Fleet and the Air Force would probably stand ready to evacuate the various military men, province chiefs, district chiefs, ministers, and deputies who have been co-operating with us—whether they go to Thailand or are airlifted to Taiwan, the Philippines, Hawaii, or straight to the United States. In other words, the U.S. would look after those who are most able to look after themselves.

And what about the bourgeois intelligentsia, who are relatively few but who really are, for the most part, opponents of

Communism, though not necessarily in sympathy with the United States? Some of them, doubtless, will go into exile; others will prefer to stay and make terms with the NLF—signs of this are already evident, not only in the Saigon Assembly but among middle-of-the-road exile groups abroad. There are also the various sects and splinters of sects, Buddhists, Hoa Haos, Cao Daists, who are unlikely to choose exile in large numbers but who can be expected to survive as groups despite their religious commitments, just as Catholics and their priests have in the North.

This leaves the hamlet chiefs, village chiefs, schoolteachers, policemen who have collaborated with the Americans in pacified areas. Many of these people are in the same situation as the "little people" on the American payroll. That is, they have collaborated for non-political reasons, out of a natural wish to go on being schoolteachers, policemen, etc. But, having done so behind the American shield, they live in fear of the Viet Cong. Among the small local bureaucracy there are also convinced opponents of Communism and admirers of American power—of an eager-beaver type found all over the world. Most of these fully expect to be massacred if the Americans go and at the same time, masochistically, they place small reliance on American promises to stay. They see themselves being hacked to pieces, decapitated, along with the non-politicals, who are not quite so sure of their fate.

Indeed, a certainty as to what will happen in the event of a Viet Cong "take-over" is the principal article of faith in the anti-Communist credo. One is against Communism because one *knows* that Communists massacre whoever is against them. For example, a Jesuit father back from a long residence in Vietnam recently *guaranteed* me that two million people would be slaughtered if the NLF came to power—he did not say how he had arrived at this figure; his first estimate had been three million but he had knocked a third off as a concession to my disbelief. "You mean you *think* so, Father." "No, I *know* it," he replied with fervor. Only God knew the future, I reminded him, but he did not seem to agree.

To be fair, the missionary priest was reflecting, quite accurately, middle-class attitudes in Vietnam. The *fear* of the Viet Cong is a reality in the South. To an outsider, this graphic and detailed certainty appears phobic, the product of an overworked imagination. Eyewitness and secondhand accounts of Viet Cong terror are magnified and projected into the future, as though guerrilla warfare could be expected to *intensify* in the absence of an armed enemy. In Saigon one evening I talked to a group of twenty or so students who all seemed to be living in a fantasy, fed on atrocity stories, of what would happen to them if the Americans left. A New York *Times* reporter asked them what they were so afraid of: they were young, they were specialists; a Communist government would need their skills as engineers, teachers, doctors. . . . They were bewildered by what was plainly a totally new idea; it had not crossed their minds that their training could make them useful to their class enemy. They only thought of being shot, decapitated, etc. All these young people, with one exception, were Northerners, and it had not occurred to them either what this meant in terms of their persistent nightmare: contrary to their preconceptions, they were alive and whole, having been allowed to escape, with their parents, from the jaws of Communism back in 1954.

If it had been revealed to me in a vision that two million people would die as a consequence, I suppose I would not—lightheartedly, as Mrs. Trilling thinks—propose unilateral American withdrawal. The awful fact of having had the vision would lay their deaths squarely at my door. So I would try to hammer out some "solution," *e.g.*, a new partition of the already partitioned country—a notion already hinted at in J. K. Galbraith's *How to Get Out of Vietnam;* mindful of the loyal Vietnamese, he wonders whether Saigon could not be made a free city, on the model, presumably, of Danzig or Trieste, not good precedents when you come to think of it. But what about simple annexation of South Vietnam? This would require a million troops, the expedition of Free World colonists, private investment in factories and power plants, but it would have the advantage of *imposing* democratic institutions on the South Vietnamese; moreover, the war could be moderated in view of the fact that it would now be taking place on U.S. soil, destroying U.S. property and property-holders; if we concentrated on the task of development, we could seal the frontier, stop bombing North Vietnam—a waste of time—and even interdict napalm.

Short of annexation—a fifty-first state—no solution comes to mind that could give ironclad *permanent* protection to untold numbers of anti-Communists. All current proposals, starting with Johnson's at Manila, envision an eventual departure from the scene. If we do not want to extend the boundaries of the U.S., we are left with no alternative but to extend the war, *i.e.*, continue it along present lines, regularly escalating until all resistance has been eliminated or until our computers tell us that two million and one innocent persons have been killed—at that point the war would no longer be "worth it," and we could quit with a clear conscience.

Mrs. Trilling says that she opposes the war, but logically, in her own terms, she shouldn't unless she looks on the slaughter of millions of democrats as the lesser evil. She is also troubled by the threat to the right of protest that an American withdrawal would imply. No doubt it would, yet the lack of a right of protest in South Vietnam at this very minute is not a threat but a reality, as anybody should know from reading the papers. Americans are free to criticize the war in South Vietnam; the South Vietnamese are not. Admittedly, there is more diversity of opinion in the South on this subject than there is, probably, in the North, yet in neither place is there any real freedom of the press or of public debate.

For anybody but a pacifist, the balancing of means against ends in wartime is of course a problem, which can be real or false, depending on whether the end to be obtained is visible and concrete or merely conjectural. If it were known that Ho Chi Minh was sending millions of Catholics or members of ethnic minorities to gas chambers, there would be a real dilemma for intellectuals and non-intellectuals, too, as to how much force and what kind should be applied to stop him, whether napalm, phosphorus, magnesium and cluster bombs should be used against his population, whether his "sanctuaries" in Cambodia and China should be invaded. . . . But no one outside the Administration pretends that Ho is Hitler. Mrs. Trilling's tone suggests that she thinks he is Stalin, yet would she reproach U.S. intellectuals, herself included, for having failed to seek an "answer" to save the millions who perished in Stalin's prisons and slave-labor camps? Like the Bertrand Russell of the epoch, did she conscientiously *weigh* dropping an atom bomb?

There are no "answers" except in retrospect, when the right course to have followed seems magically clear to all. At present nobody can produce a policy for Vietnam that is warranted by its maker to be without defects. Quite aside from Communism, this is a civil war, and civil wars customarily end with a bloody settling of scores, because of the fratricidal passions involved and also for the obvious reason that the majority of the losers have nowhere to escape to; it is their country, too. But one can fear this for Vietnam whichever side wins. What safeguards exist for the Viet Cong and its millions of sympathizers and dependents if a victorious U.S. Army turns their disposal over to the ARVN—its cynical practice up to now? Does that not worry Mrs. Trilling? We *know* that the ARVN tortures its prisoners and executes civilians suspected of working with the VC. Despite the promises of the Open Arms program the VC, too, may anticipate a massacre if it definitively lays down its arms. Unlike the Jesuit missionary who "hadn't seen it in the paper," the VC must have heard about the recent anti-Communist coup in Indonesia, rejoiced over by American officials (who give our Vietnamese policy credit for it); it was followed by the *execution* of 500,000 Indonesians, and the unrecorded carnage is reckoned at two million.

Yet civil wars in modern history have not invariably ended with horrible mass reprisals, above all in Communist countries.

Take the Hungarian Revolution, which was a mixture of civil war and foreign occupation. To everyone's surprise, very few were killed in the aftermath, and an *increase* in general liberty followed. Or take the Communist seizure of Poland after World War II, when two Polish armies fought each other, one being backed by the Russians. It was not succeeded by a bloody purge; the virtue of Polish Communism, they say, is that *no one* was executed for political opposition even under Stalinism— Gomulka went to jail. Or take North Vietnam itself, after the French defeat; here, too, there was an element of civil war, since many Vietnamese fought on the side of and supported the French. Yet under the Geneva Accords, the North Vietnamese with minor exceptions did not interfere—sometimes even assisted—while 860,000 persons were evacuated (including 600,000 Catholics) by the French Army and the Seventh Fleet. It is true that the emigrants lost their property and that in the agrarian reform of 1955-56 numerous landowners, rich peasants, and others were executed—Bernard Fall quotes an estimate of 50,000. I do not have, for purposes of comparison, statistics on those who died in Diem's agricultural "experiment"—the Strategic Hamlets program—and if I had, it would not alter the ineluctable fact of 50,000 deaths. It is possible that this could repeat itself in South Vietnam, if collectivization is attempted. Against this is the fact that the mistake was recognized and amends made where still possible (The Rectification of Errors Campaign), and the point about an acknowledged mistake is not to repeat it.

The Hungarian and Polish examples suggest that if opposition is widespread in a Communist state a conciliatory policy is pursued; the turnabout in North Vietnam in 1956, when resistance to the land-reform purges led to open rebellion, further illustrates the point. If, on the other hand, opposition is confined to a minority, that minority is dealt with ruthlessly. Let us assume this principle applies: Mrs. Trilling should be reassured if she is confident that opponents of Communism in Southeast Asia can be counted in the millions. But if she overestimates their numbers, then indeed she has grounds for alarm. On the other hand, if they are relatively few—say, in the hundreds of thousands—evacuation ought not to present insuperable difficulties. As for their readjustment elsewhere, one cannot be sanguine. Nevertheless, here, too, there are precedents: the United States has been able, for instance, to absorb 300,000 escapees from Castro's Cuba—a statistic not usually remembered in this kind of discussion.

Of course this little principle, whatever comfort it may offer, is not a "law." Nor is evacuation of a whole minority of oppositionists imaginable except in a blueprint. Some would miss the boat. Let us suppose that whatever happens, a thousand will be left behind, to be tried and executed by People's Tribunals or cut to ribbons in their hamlets. Or a hundred. Or only one. It is the same. Mrs. Trilling would have his death on her conscience. She condemned him to die by her opposition to the war. She failed him. We all failed him. We ought to have thought harder—that is Mrs. Trilling's attitude. But we condemn thousands of people to death every day by not intervening when we could—read the Oxfam ads. Or the appeals in the morning mail; yesterday I condemned someone to die of muscular dystrophy. I judged some other cause "more important." Not to mention

my own comforts and pleasures. I am calloused. Everyone
today who is well off is calloused, some more, some less. This
has always been the case, but modern means of communication
have made it impossible not to know what one is *not* doing;
charitable organizations are in business to tell us all about it.
When Mrs. Trilling reproaches me as an intellectual for my lack
of moral concern, she makes me think of the Polish proverb
about the wolf who eats the lamb while choking with sobs and
the wolf who just eats the lamb.

What Mrs. Trilling wants is a prize-winning recipe for stopping the war and stopping Communism at the same time; I
cannot give it to her. Nor frankly do I think it admirable to try
to stop Communism even by peaceful subversion. The alterna-
tives to Communism offered by the Western countries are all
ugly in their own ways and getting uglier. What I would hope
for politically is an internal evolution in the Communist states
toward greater freedom and plurality of choice. They have a
better base, in my opinion, than we have to start from in dealing
with such modern problems as automation, which in a socialist
state could be simply a boon.

Certainly, town planning, city planning, conservation of natural and scenic resources are more in the spirit of socialism,
even a despotic socialism, than in that of free enterprise. Today,
in capitalist countries the only protection against the middle-
aged spread of industrial society lies in such "socialistic" agencies as the Belle Arti and the Beaux-Arts, concerned with saving
the countryside from the predations of speculators and com-
petitive "developers," like real-estate developers. It seems
possible, too, that Communism will be more able to decentralize

industries through the exercise, paradoxically, of central control than the Welfare State has been. And variety of manufactures, encouragement of regional craft, ought to be easier for Communist planners whose enterprises are not obliged by the law of the market to show a profit or perish; there is no reason that "useless" and "wasteful" articles should be made only for the rich. In any case, external pressure is not going to liberalize Communist regimes; that seems to be fairly clear. It can only overthrow them or act to prevent them from taking power, with consequences that liberals, in view of Greece, Spain, Indonesia, might not be eager to "buy."

I should like to see what would happen if the pressure were taken off. What would Vietnam be like today if the United States had insisted on elections in '56 and the country had been unified by popular vote—which hindsight finally concedes might have been the best plan? Greatly daring, I should say that the best plan right now, eleven years later, might be to give the NLF a chance to enact its program. This calls for a National Assembly freely elected on the basis of universal suffrage, a coalition of classes for the reconstruction of the country, gradual and peaceful unification with the North, an independent and neutralist foreign policy. It guarantees the rights of private property and political, religious, and economic freedom. Whether this program, evidently designed to allay the alarms of the middle-class Vietnamese, is to be taken at face value, that is, whether the Front really means it, is something no one outside the Front's councils can know for certain. One can hope that it is so and fear that it is not. And even if the program, with its proffer of amnesty (and threat of punishment for those who persist in collaborating with the invader), is offered in good faith as a serious design for the future of the South, events may overtake it, *e.g.*, a right-wing rebellion, disastrous floods, a famine. . . . Yet for the Vietnamese this is the only "solution" at present available that gives any hope at all. Plans such as that of Philippe Devillers, proposing internationally supervised free elections to take place *first* in the Saigon-controlled zones (while the Americans retire to coastal enclaves) followed by *general* free elections in the whole of South Vietnam (after which the Americans would leave), amount in fact to showing a way in which the NLF program might be arrived at step by step with the co-operation of Saigon and of all interested parties.

Mrs. Trilling, doubtless, would think anybody a sucker who let himself be taken in by the promises of Communists, yet the promises of Communists sometimes correspond with their assessment of political realities: when Ho kept his word and let the emigrants go, he got rid of 860,000 opponents in one pacific stroke. Moreover, he had 860,000 fewer mouths to feed and a great deal of free land to distribute. The NLF would have the same motive to allow if not strongly to encourage the departure of oppositionists. Besides, if it is going to rebuild the country, the NLF will need co-operation from a variety of political and social groups, as well as credits, which might even come from the West, from General de Gaulle, for instance, from Sweden, Austria, Denmark, Canada.

The power of intellectuals, sadly limited, is to persuade, not to provide against all contingencies. They are not God, though Mrs. Trilling seems to feel that they have somehow replaced Him in taking on responsibility for every human event. This is a weird kind of *hubris*. In fact intellectuals and artists, as is well known, are not especially gifted for practical politics. Far from being statesmen with ubiquitous intelligence, they are usually not qualified to be mayor of a middle-sized city. What we *can* do, perhaps better than the next man, is smell a rat. That is what has occurred with the war in Vietnam, and our problem is to make others smell it, too. At the risk of being a nuisance, I reject Mrs. Trilling's call to order. The imminent danger for America is not of being "taken in" by Communism (which is what she is really accusing me of—that I have forgotten the old lessons, gone soft), but of being taken in by itself. If I can interfere with that process, I will. And if as a result of my ill-considered actions, world Communism comes to power, it will be too late then, I shall be told, to be sorry. Never mind. Some sort of life will continue, as Pasternak, Solzhenitsyn, Sinyavski, Daniel have discovered, and I would rather be on their letterhead, if they would allow me, than on that of the American Committee for Cultural Freedom, which in its days of glory, as Mrs. Trilling will recall, was eager to exercise its right of protest on such initiatives as the issue of a U.S. visa to Graham Greene and was actually divided within its ranks on the question of whether Senator Joseph McCarthy was a friend or enemy of domestic liberty.

Hanoi—March, 1968

"*Attachez vos ceintures, s'il vous plaît.*" "Fasten your seat belts." The hostess, plump, blonde, French, brown-eyed, in a light-blue smock, passed through, checking. It was funny to find a hostess on a military plane. Like the plane itself, loaded with mail, canned goods, cases of beer, she was a sort of last beep from the "other" world behind the mountains in Vientiane. Born in Hanoi, she had been making the run from Saigon with the I.C.C.—Poles, Indians, Canadians, of the inspection team—six times a month, weather permitting, for thirteen years, practically since the Geneva Accords.

As the I.C.C. plane, an obsolete non-pressurized Convair, circled in the dark above Hanoi, waiting to get the OK to land, out the window, by stretching against our seat belts, we could see tiny headlights of cars moving on the highways below and then the city all lit up like a big glowworm. In Phnom Penh, at the North Vietnamese Delegation, where they issued our visas, they had prepared us for this surprise, but it remained a surprise nonetheless. I thought of the Atlantic coast during World War II and the blackout curtains we had had to buy on the Cape —a Coast Guard order designed to foil enemy submarines. When the Convair taxied to a stop, it instantly doused its lights, though, and the hostess held a flashlight for the boarding officials to examine our papers. But then the airport, brilliant white and blazing with electricity. "You really don't have a blackout!" I exclaimed to the delegation from the Vietnamese Peace Committee who had come to meet us, with bouquets of snapdragons, pink sweet peas, pale-pink roses, larkspur, and little African daisies. A Japanese author and a journalist from a Tokyo paper were receiving bouquets, too. The Vietnamese did not know the word "blackout," and I tried *couvre-feu*. They dismissed the term "curfew" with laughter. "Passive defense!" In fact, there was no curfew of any sort in Hanoi—except the bell that rang at eleven o'clock nightly, closing the hotel bar—though there was one in Saigon. It was only when the sirens blew that the lights of the city went out and the cars and trucks halted and waited for the All Clear.

On the way from Gia Lam Airport into the city, we had our first alert—a pre-alert, really, given by loud-speakers; the pre-alert usually means the planes are sixty kilometers away; it is not till they are within thirty kilometers of the center that the sirens scream. Suddenly, still deep in the countryside, the driver braked the car; he had heard the pre-alert on his radio. He turned off the engine. I sat in the back seat, holding my bouquet in my lap and feeling quite apprehensive. On March 17, two days before, the much-feared swing-wing F-111A's had appeared in Thailand; there had been pictures of them in the Bangkok papers. The driver got out of the car. "He is looking for the shelter," one of my companions explained. "He has found the shelter," they announced a few minutes later, and we all climbed out of the car. In the moonlight, we could see the remains of a brick house, with its roof torn off; up the lane, there had been a hamlet, but now there were only indistinct masses of debris and, somewhere in the dark, the shelter, which

I never actually saw. It was enough to know that it was there.

Outside Hanoi, the driver's first job, I discovered, was to look for a shelter for the passengers whenever the alert or the pre-alert sounded. Every hamlet, sometimes every house, is equipped with a loud-speaker, and the alarm is rung out by the hamlet bell—the same bell that calls the peasants to work in the fields. When there is no hamlet nearby, a band of young soldiers, tramping along with a transistor radio, may warn you that the planes are coming. Once, in Hoa Binh Province, out in the west, I sat huddled in the car with the thin, large-eyed young woman interpreter while the driver conducted the search; he came back, and there was a quick conference in Vietnamese. "Here there is no shelter," she whispered, gravely touching my arm, as we listened to the bombs, fortunately some miles off. Though the shelter may be only a hole in the ground, the assurance that there is such a burrow handy gives a sort of animal comfort—possibly not unlike the ostrich's. Or maybe it is a grateful sense that somebody, an unknown friend, has thought about your safety; even if the uncovered earth shelter cannot protect you from a direct hit, the thought, as they say of small presents, is what counts.

In the city, there are individual cement cylinders, resembling manholes, every few feet, with round fitted covers of cement or of plaited reeds—good against fragmentation bombs. In a pinch, they will accommodate two small Vietnamese. But what happened, I wondered, if there were more people on a given street when the alarm sounded than there were shelters to hold them? As in a game of going to Jerusalem or musical chairs, who would be left outside? It is a schoolmen's problem, that of the outsider, which is posed in the scramble of extreme situations, and I was curious—anxious, even—about the socialist solution. But I never was able to observe for myself what did in fact occur: in my two and a half weeks in North Vietnam, it chanced that only once was I in the city streets during an alert and then only long enough to see the people scattering as our driver raced toward the hotel and its communal shelter. And I felt that it would be somehow impolite to express my curiosity in the form of a point-blank question; there are many questions one does not want to ask in Hanoi.

In any case, the target of the Hanoi government is one shelter per person within the city limits—I am not sure whether this ratio takes into account the communal shelters attached to institutions. During my stay, hundreds of brand-new cylinders were lying along the sidewalks, waiting for the pavement to be dug up and holes sunk to contain them, and every day trucks kept dumping more. Production and delivery were ahead of the picks and shovels. "Manufacturing shelters is one of our principal industries now," people remark, rather ruefully, watching the gray cylinders being put into place. What can be done with these grim manholes, war memorials, when and if peace comes? The only answer I could think of was to plant flowers in them.

Johnson's speech of March 31—and the subsequent eerie absence of alerts—did not cause even a momentary flagging in the shelter program. Yet, so far as I could tell, the shelters were more a symbol of determination than places to scuttle to when the planes approached. The city population had a certain disdain for using them. "There are toads in them," a pretty girl said, making a face. Like the white-gowned surgeon I met, a

Hero of Labor, who had calculated the statistical probabilities of being killed by a bomb in the night and decided that he preferred to stay in bed, to be fresh for operating the next morning, many people in Hanoi decline to leave their beds or their offices when the peremptory siren shrills; it is a matter of individual decision. Only foreign visitors are hustled to safety by their guides and interpreters and told to put on their steel helmets or their pellet-absorbent hats of woven reeds or straw. A pellet in the brain is the thing most dreaded by the Vietnamese—a dread that as a brain-worker I more than shared; unfortunately the hat they gave me was too small for my large Western head, and I had to trust to my helmet, hurriedly strapping it on as I trotted down the hotel stairs to the communal shelter and glad of the excuse of social duty to do what private fear was urging.

Your guides are held responsible by the authorities if anything happens to you while you are in their care. This applies particularly to guests invited by North Vietnamese organizations (which we were); accredited journalists are allowed more rein. I was asked not to go out into the street alone, even for a short walk, though the rule was relaxed when the bombing of Hanoi stopped on April 1—Hanoi time. This of course limited one's bodily freedom, but I accepted it, being a law-abiding person. Our hosts of the Peace Committee told us that they had been severely reprimanded because some frisky young South Americans had eluded their control last summer and roved unsupervised about the country; one got a pellet in the brain and had to be sent by plane to Moscow to be operated on; he lived. Whenever we traveled, one of the comrades of the Peace Committee made sure I had my helmet by personally carrying it for

7

me. I was never alone, except in bed or writing in my room. In the provinces, when we stayed at a guest house or came to inspect a village, each time I went to the outlying toilet, the young woman interpreter went with me as far as the door, bearing my helmet, some sheets of tan toilet paper she had brought from Hanoi, and, at night, the trusty flashlight. She waited outside till I was through and then softly led me back.

That first night, driving in from the airport, everything was novel. The driver had left the radio turned on in the car when he switched off the lights. We could hear it talking, as if to itself, as we paced up and down, and I had the foolish notion that the planes, wherever they were, might hear it, too. Other shadowy sedans and passengers were grouped by the roadside; there had been a great influx at the airport that night because for over three weeks, four times running, the I.C.C. flight had not been able to make it down the narrow air corridor from Vientiane to Hanoi. On the road we had passed several cars with diplomatic license plates, one, surely, containing the Indonesian ambassador, who had boarded the plane with his golf clubs; he used them to exercise on his lawn. Now abruptly all the headlights went on again; motors started. "They are going away. They are going away," the radio voice had said in Vietnamese; the pre-alert was over.

Activity resumed. A chattering stream of people, mostly young, was flowing along the highway from the city, walking or riding bicycles and motor bikes: boys in work clothes or uniforms, with camouflage leaves in their helmets, girls and women, some riding pillion, carrying baskets of salad greens and other provisions; now and then a wrinkled old peasant, in black, with balance-pole on shoulder or pushing a cart. A cow raised its head from a field. All that nocturnal movement and chatter gave an impression of revelry, as if a night ball game or a theater had just let out; probably a work shift had ended in the factories. Along the road's edge cases of supplies were stashed, covered with jute or tarpaulin. Jeeps and military trucks, some heavily camouflaged, were moving steadily in the opposite direction.

We were passing pretty rows of small, compact trees—perhaps pruned fruit trees; it was too dark to tell—a pre-alert to the fact that Hanoi is a shady, leafy city, like Minneapolis or Warsaw; like Minneapolis, too, it has lakes, treated as a municipal feature, with parks and promenades. The people are proud of the trees, particularly of the giant camphor, wreathed in a strange parasite with dangling coinlike leaves. Near the bombed brick house where we waited during the alert, there was a big bare blasted trunk, maybe an oak, which was putting out a few new leaves; my companions eagerly pointed them out, making sure I did not miss the symbol of resistance and rebirth. To the North Vietnamese, I soon became aware, everything is now a symbol, an ideogram, expressing the national resolve to overcome. All of Nature is with them, not just the "brother socialist countries." Nodding their heads in time with a vast patriotic orchestra, they are hearing tongues in trees, terrible sermons in stones and the twisted metal of downed aircraft. In Hung Yen Province, you eat a fresh-caught carp under a red-and-white-nylon canopy, like a billowing circus tent enclosing the whole room; it is the giant parachute of the pilotless reconnaissance plane they have shot down. Near Hanoi, in a village co-operative, raising model pigs and making handicrafts, they show you a small mute cluster bomb, olive drab, and, beside it, the mute rusty primitive soil-scratching implement the young peasant was using in the co-operative fields when pellets from the cluster bomb killed him. Visual education, they feel, for the people, and they are not afraid of hammering the lesson in. But it is Johnson, finally, they wish to give food for thought.

Growth statistics, offered everywhere, on bicycle ownership, irrigation, rice harvests, maternity clinics, literacy are the answer to "the war of destruction," which began February 7, 1965; a bombed oak putting out new leaves is a "reply" to the air pirates of the Air Force and the Seventh Fleet. All Communist countries are bent on furnishing growth statistics (it is their form of advertising), but with Hanoi this is something special, carrying a secondary meaning—defiance. On a big billboard in the city center, the number of U.S. planes shot down is revised forward almost daily in red paint—2,818, they claimed when I left, and the number keeps growing. In villages, the score is kept on a blackboard. Everything they build is dated, down to the family wells in a hamlet—a means of visibly recording progress, like penciling the heights of children, with the dates opposite, on a door. And each date has a clear significance in the story of resistance: 1965 or 1966, stamped on a well, proclaims that it was built *in spite of* the air pirates.

Hanoi, it is whispered, is going underground, digging shelters, factories, offices, operating theaters, preparing for "the worst," *i.e.*, for saturation bombing by the B-52's or even— draw a deep breath—for atom bombs, although if you mention those to one of the leaders, he tersely answers that Johnson is not crazy. This feverish digging, while dictated no doubt by a very practical mistrust of the Pentagon, seems to have a second-ary meaning, too—mythic, as though the city were an allegor-ical character. Hanoi appears to be telling its people that it is ready to go underground, harrow hell, to rise again like the rice plants from the buried seed. To a Westerner, this sounds fan-tastic, so much so that I hesitate to bring it up; after all, you can tell me, Hanoi's leaders are Marxists, and Marxists do not believe in resurrection stories.

Yet the Vietnamese folk beliefs are highly animistic; they venerate (or did) the souls of their ancestors, resting in the rice fields, and the souls of rocks and trees. Their classic relief sculpture surprises you with delicate, naturalistic representa-tions of plants, birds, animals, and flowers—much more typical of Vietnamese art than grotesque images of gods and the Bud-dha. The love of Nature is strong in their literature, too, and is found even in the "captured enemy documents" the U.S. is fond of distributing for publication. This helps explain their root—attachment to the fatherland, as every observer has noticed, going deeper than politics, into some sphere of immanence the foreigner is almost embarrassed to name—"spiritual," "re-ligious"? Much is made in the North of the fatherland's sacred, indivisible unity, and, despite or because of a history of parti-tions like Poland's, the sentiment of being one country seems to be authentic and shared, incidentally, by the South Viet-namese firebrands who would like to "march on Hanoi." As a symbol of that unity, the North has planted the coconut palm;

11

the visitor may be slow to grasp the significance of this. "Coconut trees." "Yes, I see them." "Before, here in the North, we did not have the coconut tree. It is a native of Saigon."

In Hanoi you find cabbages and tomato plants growing in the ornamental garden of a museum, in parks, around an anti-aircraft unit; the anti-aircraft battery has planted a large flower garden as well and it has chickens running around the gun-emplacements. Today the abundant use of camouflage—exuberant sprigs of plants, fronds, branches, leaves of coconut and banana on helmets, anti-aircraft, military vehicles, even tied to the backs of school children—cannot be meant entirely to fool the enemy overhead. For one thing, the foliage on the anti-aircraft artillery does not begin to conceal the guns' muzzles. This camouflage, snatched from Nature, must be partly a ritual decoration, a "palm" or "laurel" of prowess and connected with ancient notions of metamorphosis—pursued by a powerful enemy, you could "survive" in the verdant form of a tree. In Hanoi, the innocent protective mimicry of coconut leaves "disguising" military hardware always made me think of Palm Sunday in a Catholic country and the devout coming out of church with palm leaves or olive branches—a pre-Easter mood. In the country, a column of army trucks and half-tracks proceeding under its thatch of greenery made me feel that Birnam Wood was rolling on to Dunsinane: "Your leavy screens throw down,/ And show like those you are."

The determination of Hanoi appears at first incredible—legendary and bizarre; also disturbing. We came eventually to the pontoon bridge, floating on bamboo, the replacement, for automobiles, of the Paul Doumer Bridge that still hangs, half bombed, like a groping tentacle, over the Red River. On the bridge, the traffic goes single file, and you wait for the oncoming cars to finish their turn before a policeman gives you the signal to advance. This waiting in line by the river's edge is scary—there has been a lot of bombing in the area, as you can see by looking around—and it is even scarier when you start across the frail, wavy bridge; traffic moves very slowly, with many halts, and if the bombers should come while you are there, suspended over the water, there would be no escape; useless to look for shelters on the insubstantial bridge, obviously, and you could not jump into the dark, quite swift river. You just have to put your mind on something else, make conversation; I always dreaded this crossing, the sense of being imprisoned in a metal box, a helpless, all-but-motionless target, and I had the impression that the Vietnamese did not care for it either; each time, there was a general easing of tension when the bridge was finally negotiated.

In the hotel, to my stupefaction, there was hot water, plenty of it. During nearly a month spent in South Vietnam the year before, I had had *one* hot bath—on the U.S.S. *Enterprise*. In my room at the Continental in Saigon, there was only cold water, and when I was once offered a bath in the room of a New York *Times* correspondent, the water ran dark red, too rusty to get into. In theory, they had hot water in the Marine Press Base at Da Nang, but in practice they didn't. Other luxuries I found at the Thong Nhat Hotel were sheets of toilet paper laid out on a box in a fan pattern (keys at the desk were laid out in a fan pattern, too), a thermos of hot water for making tea, a package of tea, a teapot, cups and saucers, candies, cigarettes, and a mosquito net draped over the bed and tucked in; in Saigon, I had been tortured by mosquitoes.

It was obvious that the foreigners at the Thong Nhat lived better than the general population, but this could be said, too, of the foreigners at the Continental, who moreover had to pay for what they got, whereas in Hanoi a guest of a Vietnamese organization was not allowed to pay for anything—I never had to change so much as a dollar bill into dongs. The knowledge of living much better than others (the meals were very good) and at the expense of an impecunious government whose food-production areas were being pounded every day by my government produced a certain amount of uneasiness, which, however, wore off. There was nothing to be done about it anyway, and I soon was able to verify that outside no families were sleeping in the streets, as they had been in Saigon, nobody was begging or in rags, and the people appeared healthy, though tired in some cases, particularly those who were old and had doubtless been hungry a good part of their lives.

On opening the window, I found that there was an extraordinary amount of traffic, extremely noisy traffic, though nobody in Hanoi owns a private car—only bicycles and motor bikes. The honking of horns and screeching of brakes went on all night. To someone who lives in a European city where it is against the law to honk your horn, the constant deafening noise seems very old-fashioned. My ears had forgotten those sounds, as they had forgotten the clanging of streetcars and the crowing of cocks at 4:00 A.M. Hanoi still has both cocks and streetcars, and you can hear the whistle of trains, as well as the more up-to-date noise of MIGs overhead and the almost continuous voice of the loud-speakers, invariably feminine and soothing, sugared, in tone. Unless you know Vietnamese, you cannot guess whether they are announcing an air raid or telling you the planes have left or simply giving a news broadcast or a political diatribe.

There is a good deal in North Vietnam that unexpectedly recalls the past. Waiting to cross the Red River recalled my first trip to Italy, just after World War II, when most of the bridges were down ("Bombed by the Liberators," in Italian, was scrawled all over the devastated cities and towns) and our bus crossed the Po or the Adda on a tremulous pontoon bridge; the loud-speaker outside the hotel window ("Attention, citizens, attention") recalled the loud-speakers in Florence during a spring election campaign (*"Attenzione, cittadini, attenzione"*). Jouncing along a highway deeply pitted by pellets from cluster bombs made me think of my childhood: bumpy trips in northern Minnesota; Grandma in a motoring hat and duster; and how each time we struck a pothole her immense white head, preceded by the hat, would bounce up and hit the car's canvas top. North Vietnam is still pioneer country, where streams have to be forded; the ethnic minorities, Meos, Muongs, and Thais, in the mountains of the wild west, though they do not wear feathers, recall American Indians. The old-fashioned school desks and the geometry lesson on the blackboard in an evacuated school, the kerosene lamps in the villages, the basins of water filled from a well to use to wash up before meals on an open porch, the one- or two-seater toilets with a cow ruminating outside brought back buried fragments of my personal history. I was

15

aware of a psychic upheaval, a sort of identity crisis, as when a bomb lays bare the medieval foundations of a house thought to be modern.

The daytime alerts in the hotel reminded me very much of fire drill in school. During my stay there was no bombing near the hotel, though the siren sometimes sent us to the shelter as often as six times in twenty-four hours. After a while you estimate the distance of the explosions you hear—six kilometers, ten, fifteen—and you think you can tell the dull, resounding noise a bomb makes from the crackle of ack-ack. In the hotel, I began to have a feeling of security, like the veteran correspondents who usually did not bother to get up during night raids or who, if they were up already, wandered out into the street to watch the anti-aircraft activity. In the daytime, it became a slightly tiresome routine to walk, not run, to the shelter, where a delegation of Chinese in gray uniforms—who never spoke to anyone—were always the first arrivals, and wait for the All Clear. And as in the case of fire drill, I began to half wish for some *real* excitement, for the bombs to come a bit nearer and make a louder bang. It got to be a disappointment if the alert was a false alarm, *i.e.*, when you simply sat in the shelter and heard no action at all. The other foreigners must have felt the same way, for when the explosions were noisy and the guns replied, the conversation in the shelter became much livelier, and there were giggles.

An alert was also a social event; you saw new faces and welcomed back old friends—that is, people you had known a few days—reappearing from a trip to Haiphong or Nam Dinh. One day in the shelter I met the Danish ambassador to Peking, and

16

another time a whole diplomatic dinner party, men in dark suits, large, freshly waved ladies from the bloc countries in low-cut silks and satins, an Indian lady in a truly beautiful blue sari, joined us drab "regulars" on the underground benches, having left their double rows of wine glasses and their napkins on the table of the hotel's private dining room, reserved for parties— this eruption, as of a flight of butterflies, was a momentary wonder in our somewhat mothy, closet-like existence.

The late-night alerts were different. Though I had concluded that there was no real danger of bombing in the immediate neighborhood of the hotel—unless Johnson escalated again, with B-52's or "nukes," in which case my personal survival was not of any interest; I would not care to survive—at night, when the shrilling of the siren waked me, I forgot and would jerk up from the pillow with my heart pounding, grope my way out of the mosquito netting, find the flashlight in the dark, slippers, dressing gown, et cetera, and stumble, still unnerved, down the stairs and out through the hotel garden, pointing my flashlight down, searching for the entrance to the shelter. Those late-March night raids made everybody angry. According to the Vietnamese, who were experts on such matters, they consisted of one or two planes only, whereas before they had come in large purposeful waves; their object now must be psychological—without any military pretext—to harass the population at random, deprive it of sleep, while at the same time lessening the risk to themselves of being shot down, for it is harder to hit a single plane in the sky than to pick off one or two out of a serried dozen or twenty.

No planes, so far as I know, were shot down over Hanoi during my stay, though one, they said, an Intruder, had been shot down the day of our arrival. The foreign correspondents agreed that the bombing was slowing down, at least in the region of Hanoi, and they wondered whether the Americans could be short of planes, on account of the number destroyed or damaged in the late-January Têt offensive. The date of manufacture stamped on a shot-down plane was always of great interest; if a plane manufactured in July was shot down in August, this suggested that stocks were low.

In fact, though we did not know this in Hanoi, the "return" of the bombing, in dollars terms, had been added up early in the year by the accountants in Washington. The April number of *Foreign Affairs* was revealing that it had cost the U.S. six billion dollars to destroy an estimated 340 million dollars' worth of facilities: clearly a low-yield investment. The cost in lives of U.S. pilots in comparison with estimated North Vietnamese losses seems not to have been computed—where, on the balance sheet, would the lone target, working in a rice field, of an anti-personnel bomb figure? Left out of the calculations also— surely an oversight?—was the cost to the North Vietnamese government of the shelter program, not to mention the cost of the loud-speakers and the personnel to man them.

Only once in the city while I was there did a bomber "sneak through" the warning system. It happened once in the country, but there it was less spectacular to hear the thud of bombs be-fore, so to speak, listening to the overture of the sirens; in the country, as I said, there are no sirens anyway and surprises were to be expected. In Hanoi, it happened one evening at the

Museum of War Crimes, when we were sitting down to little cups of tea at a long table following a tour of the exhibits. Suddenly, there was a long-drawn-out, shrill, banshee-like, shrieking noise, succeeded by a shattering explosion. At the same time, out the window, we could see a plane streak across the sky. The museum director, an officer in uniform, rushed us out into the garden; guiding me by the arm, he was propelling me toward the shelter. Big red stars looking like skyrockets were bursting in the dark overhead. Then the siren must have blown, though I have no memory of hearing it. In the museum's shelter, we heard more bombs exploding. "The museum is near the bridge," the interpreter murmured, as if to excuse the fact that a raid had come so close. When the All Clear sounded, we went in and found the tea cold in our cups. Back at the hotel, during the next alert, one of the guests told us that there had been three bombs and a Shrike.

To return from a shelter to a disarrayed table where the tea has grown cold in the cups and resume a conversation at the precise point it had left off ("You were saying . . . ?") is a daily, sometimes an hourly, occurrence in the North—inevitably so, since tea is served visitors on every ceremonious occasion, and all occasions, however sickening or painful, are ceremonious. Hospitality requires that tea should be served at the beginning and end of any visit: tea, cigarettes, candies, and long slender little cakes that taste of bananas. The exceptions were the Journalists' Union and the War Crimes Commission, both of which served beer, and the prison where the captured pilots were held, which offered a choice of beer or a soft drink, plus bananas. I could never make out the reason behind these slight variations of an otherwise inflexible precept. It was easy to guess why beer was served to journalists (newsmen drink), while the Writers' and Artists' Union served tea, but why beer at the War Crimes *Commission* and tea at the War Crimes *Museum?* Maybe beer is more expensive, and Mr. Luu Quy Ky of the Journalists' Union and Colonel Ha Van Lau of the War Crimes Commission had bigger budgets than the others. In some instances, tea was followed by coffee.

Perhaps I should have asked, but the Vietnamese are sensitive, and to wonder aloud why beer was served instead of the customary tea might have been taken, I thought, as a criticism of the hospitality: "Why did they *not* serve tea?" In the same way, I was reluctant to ask why in some co-operatives, factories, and associations there were portraits of Marx, Engels, Lenin, Stalin, and Ho, while in others there was only Ho. Was it a matter of personal preference on the part of the administrator? That did not appear likely. Once, in a village co-operative I thought I saw Marx, Engels, Lenin, and Ho, and no Stalin— which made a joyful impression on me—but when I got up from my chair, I found that Stalin had been behind me all along, chuckling. The explanation may be that if the center you are visiting is a branch headquarters of the Lao Dong (Workers') Party, you get the whole pantheon; otherwise, only Ho. The absence of portraits of Mao and of the current Soviet leaders seemed self-explanatory ("Vietnam asserts its independence"), but it could not be remarked on, any more than you can remark to a host on the absence of certain persons who you might have thought would be invited to a party.

In the War Crimes Museum, that evening, among the exhibits they had showed us a Shrike, so that the sudden advent of the live missile had the air, to us, of a coincidence ("Speak of the devil . . ."), but of course, to the North Vietnamese, nearly all the exhibits in the museum "matched" what was befalling them regularly. The museum, unlike that at Auschwitz, is strictly contemporary. There were cluster bombs—guavas and pineapples—some of the delayed-action type, regarded as the most fiendish, ordinary placid TNT bombs of varying weights, ranging from babies of 200 to big daddies of 3,000 pounds, rockets, an assortment of missiles, crop-spraying powders (with the results in a bottle), tear gases, front and rear views of patients hit by a spray of pellets from the "mother" bomb, X rays of pellets in human skulls, photos of napalm and phosphorus victims (napalm has not been used in the vicinity of Hanoi and Haiphong, or, as the Vietnamese say, "not yet"), quite a collection of exhibits. And shuffling about among the displays was a small middle-aged Vietnamese woman in a bunched sweater, wide trousers, and sandals, who was staring, as if drawn by some morbid, fascinated curiosity, at the weapons and devices in the glass cases, at the big bombs arranged, like modern metal sculptures, on the floor; she bent to read the labels, sometimes furtively touched. They told us, lowering their voices, that she had been haunting the museum ever since she had lost her twenty-year-old son early in the year.

An American apologist might claim that she was an exhibit, too, a "plant" to invoke the sympathy of soft-headed pacifists and other bleeding hearts, but in fact the museum personnel seemed somewhat put out by her presence and by the occasional snuffling, sobbing noises she made, interrupting the scholarly presentation of the material. In short, they reacted like museum officials anywhere who were not lacking in heart but had their professional duties, which included discouraging nuts and people with "troubles" from intruding on official visits. It was true, she *was* causing our attention to stray. Then, as if guiltily conscious of being a disturbance, she would hastily quiet down and regain her composure, peering into the glass cases with an air of timid wonder, like a peasant viewing the tools of modern civilization and wondering what they were for. She seemed to be trying to put her lost son and these efficient implements together in some satisfactory manner, as though to make a connection and localize the source of her pain. Sometimes, appearing to find it for a moment, she actually smiled and nodded to herself.

She had gone, I guess, when the Shrike came. Perhaps one of the museum employees had persuaded her to go home finally or given her some tea in the kitchen. To tell the truth, when the Shrike came I forgot about her; I had got used to the fact that during an alert the ordinary Vietnamese—chambermaids, cooks, waiters, desk clerks, tea servers—vanished from sight, only to reappear when the alert was over. Either they proceeded to their own shelters, separate from those for foreign guests, or, like the chambermaids in the hotel who doubled as militia, they shouldered guns and went up to the roof, or they continued quietly with their jobs, like the cook I once glimpsed in the hotel sitting in his white apron and hat at the kitchen table when the All Clear blew. The siren was a Last Trump separating the sheep—us—from the nimble goats. At the

National Liberation Front Delegation, the distinction was marked by a heavy dark-brown curtain dividing the communal shelter between personnel, on one side, and, on the other, the Chief of Mission, his immediate staff, and his guests. To an American, such a frank distinction appears *ipso facto* undemocratic.

At the museum, in a parting ceremony, they presented us with rings made from downed U.S. aircraft. Like a wedding ring, mine is engraved August 1, 1966—the day the plane was shot down—and has the initials H. Y., which must stand for Hung Yen Province. They also gave me a woman's comb of the same material. Such souvenirs seem to be popular in Hanoi, but though, as they watched, I murmured *"Merci beaucoup"* and hurriedly, like one rapidly swallowing medicine, tried the blunt ring on my finger, I instantly slid it off and dropped it into my handbag; luckily, I had the excuse that it was a man's ring: too big. Back in the hotel, I shut it up in a drawer out of sight, but it kept troubling my mind, making me toss at night, like an unsettled score. For some reason, the comb, scalloped in the Vietnamese style, did not bother me.

Perhaps, if I had had the courage, I might have declined to take the ring, handed it back to the Vietnamese as soon as I realized what it was. As my grandmother tried to teach me, one need never be afraid to say no. But from their point of view, it was a symbol of friendship, a medal pinned on my chest. They were proud to bestow it. What was it that, deeper than politeness, which was urging me to do so, made it impossible for me to keep it on my finger, even for a few minutes—just not to give offense? Maybe the premonition that if I once put it

23

on, I could never take it off; I could not sport it for the rest of my stay and then get rid of it as soon as I left the country—that would be base. Yet equally repugnant to my nature, to my identity, whatever that is, to the souls of my ancestors, would be to be wedded for life or at least for the duration of this detestable war to a piece of aluminum wreckage from a shot-down U.S. war plane. Or was it just the fact that it did not "go" with my other jewelry?

Nor could I drop it in the wastebasket of my hotel room. The chambermaids would find it and return it to me: *"Votre bague, madame."* Or, worse, they would feel that, to me, their friendship band was rubbish. But if respect for the feelings of others forbade my junking it in a wastebasket of the Thong Nhat Hotel, then there was no sea anywhere deep enough for me to drop it into. I had to keep it. The comb, presenting no problem, a simple keepsake and rather pretty, remained openly on my bureau in the Thong Nhat with my other toilet articles. Yet I now slowly realize that I never passed it through my hair. Mysterious. I cannot explain the physical aversion, evidently subliminal, to being touched by this metal. Quite a few of the questions one does not, as an American liberal, want to put in Hanoi are addressed to oneself.

The Party Car

In glaring contrast to Saigon, Hanoi is clean—much cleaner than New York, for example. The sidewalks are swept, there is no refuse piled up, and a matinal sprinkler truck comes through, washing down the streets. In the somewhat gloomy lobby of the hotel, where foreign correspondents sit conferring with their interpreters, like clients murmuring with their lawyers on the benches of a courtroom, a strong smell of furniture polish rises from the worn furniture. The abundant archaic towels in the bathroom are stiff from many launderings—in cold water, probably, and a harsh soap. Sanitation is almost a fetish, imbued with political fervor: *wiping the slate clean.* In Hanoi, there are no prostitutes on the streets (the claim is that they have all been reformed), no ragged children with sores. It is rare to see a child with a dirty face, though children themselves are fairly rare, most having been evacuated to the country, where their parents visit them on weekends.

The fiercer animals in the zoo—lions and tigers—have been evacuated, too, or, rather, turned loose in the mountain forests. According to a Western news agency, the severely rationed economy could not spare fresh meat to feed them—good news for the Pentagon, since, if true, it proved that the war was "hurting." Mr. Phan of the Peace Committee, who volunteered the story, told it differently. He said they sent the dangerous animals away in case an air strike should wreck their cages and let them escape into the streets. I prefer Mr. Phan's explanation, delivered with big grave eyes. It has its amusing side, like the thought, hilarious for children, of an elephant escaping from the circus. Yet of course the problem is serious and confronts any city under bombing, just as much as what to do with the pictures in the museums. In World War II, what happened to the animals in the London Zoo? Where did they put them?

Nor—excuse me—is it unthinkable that the U.S. Navy or the Air Force would consider bombing a zoo. The model leper colony of Quyn Lap was bombed not just once—which might have been an accident—but thirty-nine times; I have seen photographs of the pandemonic scenes as doctors and attendants sought to carry lepers to safety on their backs and on stretchers —limbs wasted to stumps, arms ending in knobs. One hundred and sixty secluded buildings, housing more than 2,000 lepers, were demolished (I apologize for using North Vietnamese statistics, but the Americans have not supplied any); the first raid netted 139 dead, some, it is said, machine-gunned as they scattered. "But what could be the motive?" Americans protest. "What is the *point* of bombing a model leper colony?" I do not know the motive but I know the result: the surviving lepers have been distributed to ordinary district and provincial hospitals, where they are, to put it mildly, a problem, a pathetic menace to public health. If you bomb lepers, why draw the line at captive lions and tigers, who could be quite a menace, too?

In any case, the Hanoi government has sent the four-footed carnivores back to the wild. They are the only instances of what the U.S. calls "refugees," *i.e.*, forcibly evacuated non-belligerents, the war has created in the North. The zoo, very spruce, with well-swept paths, now contains chiefly sage monkeys, intelligent chimpanzees, and, for disgust, some cruel vultures, whose cage, at feeding-time, is the star attraction; maybe for Communist citizens (I cannot forget the monstrous sated vultures of the zoo in Warsaw), they are a fascinating object lesson in insensate, ruthless greed.

Unlike the half-evacuated zoo devoted mainly to peaceful herbivores, the city of Hanoi, like a dragon, breathes fire at every corner. Besides the shelters, the anti-aircraft, the scoreboard of shot-down airplanes, the army trucks, the boys and girls in uniform, there are huge war posters everywhere, graphics of Liberation Front heroes, slogans; the current attraction at the movie houses is a story about the heroine of Ham Rong (Dragon's Jaw) Bridge, the beautiful leader of a militia unit in Thang Hoa Province, pictured on colossal billboards with helmet and rifle.

Some writers have pictured Hanoi, even before the air war, as drab, and this is true today, certainly, of the old mercantile streets, which nobody could think of as colorful. There is almost nothing to buy except, literally, hardware: *e.g.*, flashlights, thermoses, secondhand bicycles, and bicycle parts. Many shops are closed down. The principal private businesses seem to be barbershops and bicycle-repair shops. The very name Silk Street sends a pang through the luxury-loving passer-by. In Hung Yen Province, there are still mulberries and silkworms, but their product presumably goes for export. Cotton dress goods and woven table mats made by co-operatives are sold in the government department store. As in all Communist countries, books are cheap, but the shelves and counters of the Hanoi bookstores display, almost exclusively, textbooks of one sort or another: technical, scientific, political. Little fiction or poetry, and that mostly of an edifying or patriotic character; few translations of foreign classics, except Marx and Engels. The translation of modern European and American authors, a thriving industry in Poland, Czechoslovakia, Yugoslavia, is here still largely a dream for the future: "We have started to translate your progressive writers: Jack London and Mark Twain."

In the street, the population, riding its bicycles, is dressed in somber colors: black trousers, white shirt or blouse; khaki, gray, or navy blue zipper jackets. A few very old pedicabs or Cyclopousses, trembly relics of inequality, still circulate, usually as delivery carts, though occasionally you see a passenger aboard—a stout middle-aged woman with bundles. The alluring, transparent ao-dai, still the normal dress of women in the South, is worn here only by performers or by élite workers on occasions of welcome. It was startling to visit a generator factory and be received, with bouquets of gladiolas, by a bevy of young women dressed in bright ao-dais and with big red Cupid's bows, reminiscent of the twenties in America, painted on their lips. Assembled at the factory entrance, coloring shyly through the disks of rouge on their cheeks, they looked like bridesmaids emerging from a church. Ordinarily the women wear no make-up, and the only notes of color on the flying bicycles are supplied by girls' plastic rain capes, robin's-egg blue or pink. Despite the rainy winters, the umbrella, I was told, was discarded when the air war began. Mine attracted attention, and I began to be embarrassed by it, as though it had been a parasol. When not in work clothes, the men of Hanoi dressed neatly in Western suits, clean white shirt, and tie.

Hanoi is clean but defaced and stained, reminding one of a bathtub that has been scrubbed with an abrasive powder till the finish has worn off. Outside the old French residential quarter, which includes diplomats' houses, the presidential palace and gardens, and the colonnaded Ba Dinh Assembly, the buildings have not been "kept up" or renovated. Like the ancient elevator in the hotel, manufactured in Saigon in some other eon, and the sighing old French plumbing upstairs, shops, dwellings, and offices are survivors, veterans. The Catholic families who "followed the Holy Virgin south" after Geneva would not find many changes, except those wrought by time. A clubwoman I knew in Saigon, when she heard I might go to Hanoi, begged me to go and look at "her" drugstore, just as a dispossessed *ci-devant* baron might beg you to go look at "his" castle: "It is still there, my drugstore—on the Place du Marché." I understood the pilgrimage, and the drugstore was there, all right, seemingly just as she had left it in 1954; only it needed new paint and shutters. The former U.S. consulate now flies the flag of the National Liberation Front Delegation; they have changed the official pictures in the reception room and built a shelter in the garden, but otherwise it still looks very much like any U.S. consulate in the South, minus the sandbags and the Marine guards.

The only important new building is the big empty Polytechnic University, finished just before the bombing started; classes had hardly begun when they had to be dispersed to the country, and this, no doubt, was taken as a sharp lesson. Hanoi, quite naturally, is closing down existing structures rather than adding to them. The central market is closed— too dangerous an assembly point—and peasant women sell flowers, fruit, and vegetables from little stands on the sidewalks. So far as I could see, repairing bomb damage was the only build-ing activity going on in the city and its environs. If the damage is extensive, as in the case of blocks of workers' apartments badly hit (I saw them) in the suburbs, what is left of the build-ings is simply condemned, for the time being, and nobody is supposed to live there, though in reality a few families do. If it is just a question of repairing a roof, this is done rapidly.

In the Two Sisters district, an outlying section of Hanoi, on the morning of March 28, I watched workmen repairing the roof of the Church of the Little Flower; it had been bombed on March 8, at 7:50 P.M. The congregation was at evening mass when the officiating priest heard the alert on the loud-speaker just outside the church; the bombers were forty kilometers off. He ordered the congregation to disperse, and nobody who had been in church was hurt except the statues on the altar and along the walls; St. John the Baptist, in a loincloth, with his rustic cross made of sticks, and a green polychromed angel were still recognizable, though headless; the Stations of the Cross were completely shattered. Near the Gothic-style church—stone, with many crockets—there were five big bomb craters, one filled with water, among the growing market crops. Eighteen bombs, the people said, had been dropped on this Catholic hamlet, remote from the main highway and from any discernible mili-tary target. Those who had gone to mass had been lucky. Eight people were killed, and eight wounded; fifteen houses had been razed. Yet already the rubble had been cleaned up—only a child's crib had been overlooked—and once the bomb craters were leveled off and replanted, a visitor would never guess what had happened unless he were shown photographs at the War Crimes Commission.

In the center of Hanoi, where raids took place in August and again in October last year on two thickly populated city blocks (the "industrial" targets being a small hardware store and a little bicycle-repair shop), you stand deep in rubble, amid twisted bedsprings; your guides point out where a partly destroyed house has been rebuilt, looking no newer—to your eyes—than the adjacent houses that escaped. Here there is no question of urban renewal. A patch of roof or wall is hastily applied to the old worn fabric of the city. Somehow, in Hanoi I missed seeing the bombed area visited by Harrison Salisbury and others, though from their description it must have been not far from the hotel. Maybe it has been rebuilt and blends, like camouflage materials, with the emaciated buildings around it. In Hanoi and its suburbs, I noticed, only relatively fresh bomb damage is called to the visitor's attention. The rest is documentation: museum material.

Despite the shade trees, lakes, and parks, Hanoi in peacetime could undoubtedly seem drab—a poor relation of the Western Communist capitals with their tourist attractions of rebuilt palaces, restored glittering churches, picturesque market places, pretty girls in miniskirts, shops full of "good design" handwoven rugs and embroidered place mats to take home. What makes the difference, now, is the militancy, the flame in the eyes, which sometimes darts out if you make an imprudent comparison. As a common purpose, repelling the invader is a more enlivening goal, it would appear, than building socialism, a sometimes zestless affair; here, building socialism is not just an end, which may seem to be perpetually receding, like a mirage, but a *means*; the reason for making sacrifices is clear and present to everyone. In Hanoi, you do not see the dispirited milling restless crowds of the cities of Eastern Europe; almost everybody here is in a hurry. Obviously there must be discontented people, grumblers, but where are they? There cannot be a government decree ordering them to stay in their houses. Yet wherever you go, you are met with smiles, cheers, hand clapping. Passers-by stop and wave to your car on the road. Once in a while, it is true, in a poor, historically "disadvantaged" province, you pass old black-clad peasants, with cross, obstinate faces, who do not raise their eyes—like people refusing to salute a flag—as you go by, smiling and raising dust. But this is almost reassuring; unanimity would be too abnormal.

In Hanoi, because of the war, the population goes to work at six in the morning. The stores open at five or even four. Few people eat at home any more or in restaurants. They take their meals in the government canteens, turning over their rationing tickets. An exception was Mr. Phan of the Peace Committee, a gourmet, who did his own cooking, his wife being either at work in a government office, in one of her two evening classes, or at committee meetings. He profited from trips to the country to shoot birds to bring home; so, in fact, did the driver.

It was plain that life in Hanoi was austere and strenuous,

though every effort was made to lessen this for the foreign visitor, who was regarded as a weaker vessel. The indulgences of the West were known to the North Vietnamese by repute, though their travel had usually been confined to attending congresses in Communist countries. They would apologize for the inconvenience caused by the alerts—an excess of courtesy when speaking to an American, I felt. They were solicitous about one's health, how one had slept, whether one was tired. Our tour of the recent bomb sites in the city required a 7:00 A.M. departure from the hotel, and they excused themselves for this. "We are sorry about it, but that way it is safer." The bombers, they told us, seldom arrived before 9:00 A.M. "You mean the pilots have to have a hot breakfast first," I said ironically. "We do not know the explanation," they replied. "But we have observed that this is the case." It did indeed appear to be so, as a general rule, in the countryside as well as in the city. In my notes I have marked down only one early-morning alert: at 5:45 A.M. on March 21.

For an overnight trip, you waited till late afternoon to start. Preparations were methodical. First, you were given time to rest in your room. Then a light supper was ordered in the dining room for precisely four-thirty. Your guides from the Peace Committee (it was never clear whether they themselves had eaten or whether they ever rested) were distressed, almost alarmed, if you protested at eating so early, having finished lunch at about two—luckily, I am docile about sitting down to table when told to. At the destination, you would be fed again— fed and fêted. Wherever you went, there would be basins of hot water and towels for you to wash up; I was never invited to wash so often as in North Vietnam. And, when we stopped en route, young Mrs. Chi of the Peace Committee whispered: "Would you like to make water or shit?"

Each departure, smacking of danger, was an adventure. Shortly before six, the baggage waiting in the hotel lobby was carried out to the cars. In Vietnam, it gets dark about seven, all year round. By the time we went through the military check-point at the city limits (all automobiles entering or leaving the city are checked, but not bicycles or pedestrians), it was dusk, and trucks and military vehicles, which had been parked by the roadside, had begun moving, too, like sleepers awaking and stretching. This crepuscular stirring at nightfall, when good people should be preparing for bed, was full of excitement, half-childish, as though you were in a dense forest when the owls and other night creatures came into their own, and the effect was enhanced by the sibilant leaves of the camouflage. Gradually, headlights blinked on, the big trucks using only one, like the Cyclops. Lanterns hung over the tables of little country inns; a dim crowd of working people was waiting by the road's edge. "A bus stop." Under cover of darkness, the country was resupplying.

Respecting that cover, I never asked exactly what was in the trucks or where the convoys were going. I did not want to feel like a spy. Indeed, I had a strong desire not to observe any movement of men or vehicles that might have a military or political significance. I tried to restrict myself to innocent ques-tions and speculations, such as "Was that thunder and lightning or a bomb?" This inhibition extended to observing my com-panions and attempting to study their attitudes and behavior, in the manner of a social scientist. A poor approach for a reporter, but I suspect it was rather general and dictated by courtesy to a people whose country was being invaded not only by fleets of bombers but also by reconnaissance planes, monitoring every pigsty and carp pond, while in the South, below the DMZ, North Vietnamese prisoners were being interrogated, their documents, little poems, and diaries read and studied by military intelligence and U.S. political scientists, hopeful of penetrating the medulla of North Vietnamese resistance to find evidence of homesickness, malnutrition, disillusion, war fatigue.

Nevertheless, I could not help noticing an awesome lot of military traffic, any more than I could help seeing that the car I was riding in was a Volga and that the car ahead, bearing another guest of the Peace Committee, was an old Peugeot, and the car ahead of that, bearing the doctor and the photographer (guests of the government, when traveling, must be accompanied by a doctor), a Warszawa.

Nor could I wholly disconnect the intelligence apparatus within my own head, which registered the evident fact that my companions were Communists, that they were sometimes guarded in their conversation and quick to correct a doctrinal error or slip on the part of a compatriot, as when, in the Museum of Art, the director, a gray-haired painter, while making some point about a fifteenth-century Vietnamese landscape with figures, had referred in a derogatory way to the Chinese, meaning plainly, I thought, "the cruel Mings," and the Peace Committee guide, with a sharp cough, interposed, "The Chinese feudal oppressors," lest we think we had heard a slur on the People's Republic of China. The embarrassing point of this little episode, in terms of political constraint, apparent to any Westerner, including a non-Party Russian, a Czech, or a Hungarian, was probably lost on our young guide, who must have felt simply that he had covered, with smiling rapidity, a tense moment, instead of, on the contrary, causing one.

He was a nice person, Mr. Van, modest, kind, amused at himself, with a startled harelike look, always dressed, when we went to the country, in a rather sporty cloth cap and scarf. I wished he had not had to do that or to nod to us with boyish satisfaction, like a senior approving a junior recitation, when the museum director promptly echoed, "Certainly; the Chinese feudal oppressors." But I did not blame him, really. I blamed the United States. If we had not been bombing his country, Mr. Van might be a free, or at least a freer, spirit, instead of an anxious chaperon fearful that his charges might draw an "improper" conclusion.

Often, when with our friends of the Peace Committee, I thought of other Communist countries I had been to, other and different conversations. In particular of Sarajevo in the winter of 1960. I had gone to Yugoslavia on a lecture tour for the State Department—itself an index of how time has flown, politically speaking, since. Between Sarajevo, the old Bosnian capital, and Hanoi there were quite a few points in common. The flowers on arrival. When I got off the train in Sarajevo, I was too green to know that this was a Communist custom—which must have derived, I think, from pre-Revolutionary Eastern Europe—and I was amazed and flattered to find some bundled-up officials from the Writers' Union waiting for me at the station in the snow with a large bouquet of red roses. They took me to a hotel with antique plumbing, quite a different milieu from the modern hotels of Belgrade and Zagreb; the Archduke Franz Ferdinand and his wife, Sophie, had stayed there on June 28, 1914, the day they were assassinated—their names must still be in the register. Around the corner there was a sort of Museum of the Revolution, which I was immediately taken to; it was devoted to fading photos and mementoes of Princip, the assassin, and the bridge nearby, over the Miljaka River, was named for him. Strange to find that here in Sarajevo this young man, who had caused World War I and, indirectly, all its sequelae, right down through Belsen and Auschwitz, was a Hero of the People. It gave you, as they say, a different perspective, like the ubiquitous likenesses of Stalin in North Vietnam.

In Sarajevo, I was warned ahead of time, the Party apparatus was tough and illiberal. The town was poor, shabby, provincial, half-Moslem, with a bazaar and minarets; the administration was under-favored by the Tito régime. I would be meeting old doctrinaire functionaries, reactionaries in the sense of being still unreconstructed from the Stalinist period. There would be no question of the audience's understanding English, as at Zagreb or Belgrade or Ljubljana; a translator would be supplied. My lecture was on the novel, and I tried to choose examples chiefly from Russian and classical French fiction that I thought the audience might know. At the end of the lecture, the bald-headed Party literary chief rose from his chair and demanded: "Why have you not mentioned your great writer Jack London?"

This question, really an accusation, had never been leveled at me elsewhere in Yugoslavia, still less in Poland, where I had been lecturing, too. It floored me, and I could only answer, mildly, that I had never read Jack London, except a book about a dog when I was a child. The answer made the literary chief angry (like any light dismissal of somebody else's taste), but it made me popular with the translators, of whom there turned out to be two, both very young. One had studied acting in summer school at Stratford-on-Avon and had played Hamlet in a student production; the other was the son of a professor. These young men, as I soon found out, were in very bad odor with the Writers' Union, but on the occasion of my visit they had become indispensable to it, since practically nobody else in the town knew English. Probably, as in Poland at the time and in North Vietnam today, English and French, the capitalist tongues, were discouraged in the local university, offered only as "second" or optional languages, while Russian was a "first" language and compulsory—in North Vietnam, if I understood right, there is a choice between Russian and Chinese as a "first" language.

In any case, the two young men, "Hamlet"—I could not master his last name—and his friend, were making the most of my presence, to tease and annoy the Party leadership. There was a whole group of contumacious young writers, it seemed, who met in a café and discussed Greek pre-Socratic philosophers and daring writers like Nietzsche. They invited me to the café (an honor, they told me, for I was the first person over thirty ever to be admitted to their table), and naturally I went.

It was in the café, I think, that the plot was hatched to get possession of the Party car, in order to take me to the mountains and go up on the ski lift. As in Hanoi, there were no private cars in Sarajevo—certainly none for young people to ride around in. The car belonging to the Writers' Union was very old, rusty, and battered—a real heap. But to "Hamlet" and his friends, it was a prize to be captured, with some co-operation from me. In the end, they got it—virtually hijacked it, I gathered —and somehow got the gasoline, too, and we all went off to the mountain lodge, a new socialist construction, which was empty, and rode back and forth on the ski lift over the fir-tree tops, even I, who am afraid of heights. They had struck a blow for freedom; that was how they saw this escapade.

What was interesting about this group was its seriousness. They were not literary Bohemians, but deeply interested in politics and philosophy. Moreover, they were committed to Marxism and hopeful of working out for themselves, in that backward Moslem town whose chief products were pure mountain air and "Turkish" carpets, some synthesis of Marxism with more libertarian philosophies. The neo-capitalist ideas coming out of Belgrade at the time did not attract them at all, but they were curious about that intransigent figure Simone Weil, and her little book on factory work. Nor had they been infected by the careerism typical of the young big-city intellectuals of Yugoslavia, who were mostly interested in making money, acquiring unspoiled seashore property at bargain prices for vacations and watching its value mount ("We bought it for 10,000 dinars and now it's worth ten times that"), getting showy apartments and studios from the government, and staying out of trouble politically. If the literary bureaucrats of Sarajevo were the most benighted and forbidding functionaries I met in Yugoslavia, "Hamlet" and his friends were the most advanced and freest—in the true sense—young beings. A sort of polarization had taken place.

Riding along in the Volga, I wondered what had happened to them. The worst (to my mind) would be if they themselves had slowly—or rapidly—climbed up the rungs of the Writers' Union and had reached the top. The best would be if they were teaching in the university. Perhaps "Hamlet" had become a player and was treading the boards in Belgrade. Comparison with the young translators of the Peace Committee was inevitable. Their situations were equivalent: as interpreters, they had become negotiators, in a sense, between their own society and friendly elements belonging (or half belonging) to ours. And humanly they were not unalike: idealistic, pensive, patriotic, proud of their native scenery and customs. Behind the Vietnamese, however, was a grimmer life experience; young as they were, they had fought with the Viet Minh against the French. And they were still obdurately fighting, though no longer with guns. In contrast to *their* seriousness, that of the young Bosnians appeared frivolous, irresponsible; at any rate, that was how young Mr. Hieu, small-featured, slender, delicate, hardworking (he had taught himself English by listening to the BBC and the Voice of America), and his wife, Mrs. Chi, would have regarded it. And it was true: it was easier to imagine "Hamlet" and his friends giving up the struggle finally, succumbing to the local temptations—slivovitz, sloth, neo-capitalist financial "incentives"—than to imagine Mr. Hieu, Mrs. Chi, or Mr. Van surrendering principle even for a half-hour.

In an ideal world, though, Mr. Van and Mr. Hieu—and why not shy Mrs. Chi?—would be free from the inner constraints that made them circumspect with the foreigners in their charge, from the self-imposed rationing system in the realm of ideas that limited their diet to what was strictly necessary to the national interest, free to speculate, to question authority; in fact, to hijack the old Peugeot up ahead and go off on a joy ride—in a Communist country, the Party car is Father's car. But until the Americans go home, Father's car or Uncle Ho's, garaged in North Vietnam, will be treated with deferential respect. No question of "borrowing" it for private, unlicensed enjoyment. The Americans have blocked such possibilities for the young Vietnamese, and for the old, too. They have frozen the country in a posture of wary vigilance, ears pricked up for the slightest violation of the defined intellectual and political boundaries, in the same way that in the Peugeot the driver's radio, though turned low, is alert to catch an announcement from the central network of a violation of the national air space. And until the Americans go home, translation probably will be arrested at the point of Mark Twain and Jack London.

But the ideal world I am speaking of is mine, not Mr. Van's and Mr. Hieu's. I had been able to share it, to my surprise and joy, with the young Bosnians, but the North Vietnamese would reprehend the thought of our having such a libertine world in common. An irony of the war is that so little can be shared, except opposition to the American participation, by the charming Vietnamese hosts and the Americans who come here as friends—pacifists, liberals, young members of the New Left, who share among themselves an attitude of incaution and resistance to any established authority.

Hence the parable of the Party car, though it kept recurring to me during those long night trips, had to remain unspoken; I felt slightly guilty, stealthy, in confiding it even to my notes.

To begin with, any comparison to revisionist Yugoslavia would have been, automatically, odious. As the Cyclopean trucks lumbered by, bound for some destination which I did not care to know—Laos? the Ho Chi Minh Trail?—the best course was to avoid reminiscence, black out large compromising areas of my past, and concentrate on the present. A flash in the sky ahead. "Lightning, do you think?" "Maybe." A double flash. "It *looks* like lightning." "No. Bombs."

North Vietnamese Bucolic

G o out into the field," American officials last year, in blustery hectoring tones, were telling newcomers to Saigon, meaning get close to the fighting if you want to "connect" with the war. In North Vietnam, officials do not stipulate a tour of the combat zones as a condition for climbing aboard, "turning on," or, as they would express it, "participating in the struggle of the Vietnamese people." Indeed, if I had wanted to be taken to the 17th parallel, they would surely have said no: too long and dangerous a trip for a fleeting guest of the Peace Committee. And too uncertain, given the uneven pace of travel by night, in convoy, to plan ahead for suitable lodging, meals, entertainment. A reporter on the road can trust to potluck and his interpreter, but for guests hospitality requires that everything be arranged in advance, on the province and district, even the hamlet, level, with the local delegates and representatives—stage-managed, a hostile critic would say; though, if so, why the distinction between guests and correspondents? Anyway, that is how it is, and I do not feel it as a deprivation that I failed to see the front lines. The meaning of a war, if it has one, ought to be discernible in the rear, where the values being defended are situated; at the front, war itself appears senseless, a confused butchery that only the gods can understand; at least that is how Homer and Tolstoy saw the picture, in close-up, though the North Vietnamese film studios certainly would not agree.

Nevertheless, it was a good idea—and encouraged by Hanoi officials—to get out of Hanoi and go, not into the field, but into the fields. In the countryside, you see the lyrical aspect of the struggle, *i.e.*, its revolutionary content. All revolutions have their lyrical phase (Castro with his men in an open boat embarking on the high seas), often confined to the overture, the first glorious days. This lyricism, which is pulsing in Paris today as I write, the red and black flags flying on the Sorbonne, where the revolting students have proclaimed a States General, is always tuned to a sudden hope of transformation—something everybody would like to do privately, be reborn, although most shrink from the baptism of fire entailed. Here in France the purifying revolution, which may be only a rebellion, is still in the stage of hymns to liberty, socialist oratory, mass chanting, while the majority looks on with a mixture of curiosity and tolerance. But in rural North Vietnam, under the stimulus of the U.S. bombing, a vast metamorphosis, or, as the French students would say, restructuring, is taking place, not as a figure of speech, but literally. Mountains, up to now, have not been moved, but deep caverns in them have been transformed into factories. Universities, schools, hospitals, whole towns have been picked up and transferred from their former sites, dispersed by stealth into the fields; streams have changed their courses. City children have turned into peasants. Nomad tribes—horse people —thanks to irrigation projects, have been settled as farmers and equipped with bicycles. Rice has been made to grow on dry land. However this revolution may be assessed finally in terms of economic cost and yield, whether it is temporary, a mere war epiphenomenon, or can continue as a permanent experiment, the fact of it is a plain wonder. No statistics recited in an office prepare the visitor for what is, to him, in part a delightful magic show, complete with movable scenery, changes of costumes, disguises.

The Vietnamese themselves, not loath to moralize, look on it more solemnly, in terms of strictly drawn contrasts. "In the past," they say, pointing to pale-green rice fields laid out geometrically in squares and rectangles, "those fields made a crazy pattern." "Yes," I say, "like a crazy quilt," regretting, in my heart, the classic pattern of individual small-scale ownership. Mr. Phan, who likes words (he is a veteran war correspondent), nods to himself, filing the phrase away, smiles broadly. "I myself," he declares, "hate anything artificial, but I make an exception of the rice fields." We are in Hung Yen Province, flat, watery, famous for mulberries and for bees attracted by the very sweet fruit of the dragon's eye tree—the longan, which grows rank here. He makes another exception, though more doubtfully, of the ugly prefabricated honeycombs, made of paraffin and beeswax, they show us in a movie. "In the past," he says, translating the sound track, "honey production in the province was a fifth of what it is at present." "In the past" or "formerly" introduces every third sentence once you leave Hanoi. In the past, they say, this province had one small hospital; now, besides the province hospital, there is a dispensary in every village, and each district has a hospital of its own. "Formerly there was no second-level school in the entire province; now each village has a second-level school."

"In the past" and "formerly" = under the French or, in some contexts, under the old native landowners, "the cruel *lang*s."

But it is not necessary to have known the "Before" to appreciate the "After." South Vietnam, under the Americans, is a present and terrible "Before." Last year I saw the filthy hamlets there and the refugee camps. Here everything I am shown is clean. It is true that I am on an official visit, but in the South, outside of Saigon, wherever I went, I was conducted by an AID man or a U.S. or Friendly Forces officer—the exception being a tour of some refugee camps counted as "middling" by the social workers who were showing them. In the South, they cannot hide the dirt, disease, and misery. They would not know where to begin. It is true that in the North there is no fighting; a U.S. invasion might help equalize things, spreading hunger and squalor.

At any rate, in the North I saw no children with sores and scalp diseases, no trachoma (it has been almost wiped out, according to the Ministry of Health), no rotten teeth or wasted consumptive-looking frames. You do not need plague shots to visit the North, or cholera shots, for that matter. They say there is still some malaria in the northwestern mountains. In the countryside, children and young people were radiant with health; as far as I could judge, everybody under forty was in peak physical condition. Peasants and agricultural workers are favored by the rationing system and they are allowed a small percentage of land for their privately owned garden crops and animals; the difference is apparent, but not glaring—seeing them side by side with the desk workers of Hanoi, you might put it down to the difference between the country and the city, outdoors and indoors.

It was clear that in the hamlets the people had few possessions: some cooking utensils, plates and cups, bedding, a Buddhist altar with a few ornaments, one change of clothes, the small children's usually being patched and faded. The clothes in the South, chiefly army castoffs and charitable donations, were better on the whole. In the house of a peasant family in the North, you wonder at the absence of bureaus, chests, trunks, until it comes to you that they have so little to store. On the other hand, they had new-driven wells and clean outhouse toilets, sometimes one to a family, sometimes public. There was no garbage around the houses or floating in the streams. There were no smells. Pretty new brick walks led into the hamlets we visited, and a central square was often paved with brick. I remember the little *place* of the Dai Ta co-operative, under the shade of four interlacing secular banyan trees on top of which, like a tree house, a lookout tower was perched with a boy from the militia on duty; nearby was the old hamlet bell. In this particular hamlet, an old man, speaking French, dressed in faded army khakis, evidently a gentle *lang,* was grafting new varieties onto lemon trees, which wore cloth bandages where the insertions had been made. He had come out of retirement, he said, to give his aged skills to his country: under his guidance, young papaya and grapefruit trees had been planted along the walks; he indicated a Rhode Island Red rooster, scratching in the dirt, that he was trying to cross with the small local chickens to get a bigger breed.

Each hamlet and co-operative we visited boasted—and that is the word—a robust girl midwife, barely nubile herself. In the schools, we saw boys and girls with glasses, which gave them a surprisingly "Western" industrious look; I could not recall seeing a single child wearing glasses in the South. Formerly, our guides say, the peasantry was illiterate; now everyone can read and write. In fact, the Ministry of Education speaks of pockets of illiteracy remaining in the north, near the Chinese border, but the people themselves believe that they have made education universal, the young teaching the old, if necessary, husbands teaching wives. Outside the schoolhouses, though, I did not see any books in the rural areas, and indeed, as in many farm communities, reading did not seem to be practicable, on account of the early risings and bedtimes and the poor lighting—it was impossible to read a line by the tiny kerosene lamp in a province guesthouse. "Where do the people read?" I asked a woman district representative in an "ethnic" village, and the answer was: "In their offices. But mostly just newspapers. They do not have the time." She was speaking of people like herself. The peasants listen to the radio. Yet here, as in most Communist countries, there is a great hunger for books, it is said—a hunger arising partly from a former scarcity and the novelty of print.

During our travels, the one lack I felt, in comparison with the South, was the sparkle and mischief of the little boys. In the North, the children were friendly but timid, unlike the infant black marketers and bold suppliants of the South. I cannot say I *missed* having stones thrown at me or being pummeled for a cigarette, but I might have been glad to see a troop of naughty, fearless children tagging along behind us as we walked along the neat brick walks of a village co-operative, pausing to inspect a loom or a model pigsty. Here the children, even the rare show-offs, are models of conduct. A little girl, not much bigger than a doll, urged forward, entrusts her hand to mine: "Hello,

Auntie." "Auntie," for the Vietnamese, is a term of respect, like "Uncle" (hence Uncle Ho; in the Vietnamese family, the senior uncle, not the father, is the source of authority), and to call an American woman "Aunt" is an act, for a child, of extraordinary docile faith. These country people, who have never before seen an American, unless possibly a shot-down pilot, seem to accept without question the notion that there are "good" Americans—something that, in their place, lacking further evidence, I might be disinclined to believe. Never in the North did I find a woman watching me with eyes full of hatred, though this happened often in the South. Here there was only curiosity and often a desire to touch, as with a new object. Young girls would press close to me, entwine hands or arms with me, particularly when we were lined up for a photograph or to listen to a speech of welcome. The absence of a common language created a "little" language of soft gazes, smiles, caresses. Good-byes were like those at a school graduation, with parents (in this case our guides) waiting to perform the surgery of separation.

It was useful to have been in South Vietnam, to make comparisons. Yet one could have dropped from the moon into Hung Yen or Hoa Binh Province and known at once that something marvelous, in the old sense, was astir. Schools in the fields, for instance, dispersed over miles of flat landscape, hidden under thatched roofs of coconut palm or straw, so that they are almost invisible from the air. No doubt there must be historical parallels for this; I know that according to family legend, my great-great-grandfather and his brothers, denied formal education by the English, were taught their lessons by priests in the Irish wheat fields, hidden from the oppressor's view by tall rows of grain. The Irish and the Vietnamese have a bond of patriotic struggle, I was told one night at the Writers' Union by a plump, middle-aged Vietnamese poet, a troubadour or wandering minstrel, he called himself, because he had been reciting poems to the troops along the DMZ, accompanying himself on an instrument (his debased equivalent, I suppose, would be the belly dancers who minister to the Marines); when he was young, under the French colonialists, he had been in love with Irish history, he said—*"C'était ma passion"*—we talked about Parnell. But the Irish story, if true, is only a fairly tall tale, while the North Vietnamese dispersal of pupils and teachers into bamboo groves and rice fields is a living saga. The magnitude of the phenomenon, the sheer geographic spread, suggests the early Christian hermits dotted about on the Libyan Desert and in the caverns of the Red Sea.

In Hung Yen Province, you leave your cars by the roadside and walk across the dikes. A group of young teachers accompanies you; one, they say with pride, is from the South. In the North you are introduced to quite a few young people who were born on the other side of the parallel; they are the children of Viet Minh fighters who regrouped to the North in 1954 and '55. To have one of these Southerners—duskier, often, if they come from the Mekong Delta, and with round snub features, broad faces, and slightly frizzy, ashier hair—in your school or cooperative is considered a distinction: *"She* is from Bien Hoa Province, near Saigon."

Leading the way, the literature teacher, male, says politely that he gives his pupils extracts from American writers to read. "My pupils prefer Burchett, of all your authors." "But Wilfred

Burchett is an Australian. I have met him in Hanoi." Burchett is a Communist journalist who carries a North Vietnamese passport. "They like very much also *Ten Days That Shook the World*." "Yes. He was an American." Here in the Red River Delta, it has been raining heavily. Beside the flooded fields, old peasants are scooping up water, using an implement resembling a lacrosse cradle. The school huts are new, brick, with palm roofs, and set among banana trees. In the teachers' common room, there is a bust of Beethoven, awarded every year for excellence in literature. You enter a classroom, where the teacher, a thin, serious young man, is at the blackboard. The pupils rise from the desks and clap. Clapping is a mode of welcome, and the guest (if I was not mistaken) is meant to clap, too. They are having a history lesson.

Chalked on the blackboard is a map of what is evidently a military action—a battle fought against the French in 1950, Mrs. Chi whispers. This comes as a slight shock, for I do not think of that as "history" yet, *i.e.*, as classroom material. Each pupil has a textbook with photographic illustrations. Glancing over the shoulder of the young girl next to me on the school bench, I guess that it is a history of the French resistance struggle; by the end of the term, they will get to Dien Bien Phu. Today's subject, though, is not exactly history; it is a lesson in military tactics. Tapping his pointer on the map, the teacher is explaining how the Viet Minh achieved its purpose, which was to lure the French out of a fort into the forest. He illustrates his theme with anecdotes. Called on to recite, a pupil tells a funny story about the cook who got some hungry French to surrender by offering them a little rice in a saucepan. Everyone laughs.

It is a good class, attentive and lively. The girls are well dressed in long brown fitted corduroy jackets. The class age must be fifteen or sixteen; this is a second-level school, equivalent, probably, to middle high school in America. The atmosphere is reminiscent of schoolrooms in my childhood. You would not find such a well-disciplined class in America today. Yet in my school days, after World War I, we would never have been studying the tactics of Soissons or Château-Thierry. American history was the Civil War and "Remember the Maine" and the War of Independence. Maybe we "had" Gettysburg or Antietam or Chancellorsville, but I cannot remember being drilled in the tactics of those battles. The only tactics we learned, if memory serves, were Caesar's: how he built that bridge over the Rhine and caught the boats of the Veneti in his fleet's long grappling hooks. And something about Waterloo and the British square. To my mind, formed in those habits, that is still the way history *should* be taught: firmly set in the past, beyond partisan passions, and yet capable of exciting the imagination. Children in my day took sides and had heroes; you quarreled with your friends over who was superior, Napoleon or Wellington, Marlborough or Prince Eugene, Hector or Achilles. Confederate generals offered a wide range of preference: Beauregard, Stonewall Jackson, Morgan the Raider. But your heroes were not the official heroes of the nation, often the opposite; you could "like" spies and traitors: Major André and Benedict Arnold, rather than Paul Revere. Like most spirited young people, I was generally on the side of the losers. History taught, or, rather, learned, in that fashion is close to art; it is a "story."

It was too early to hope, obviously, that these embattled, endangered children could find a soft spot in their hearts for De Lattre de Tassigny, still less for the inept General Navarre. History, as taught by the French to the Vietnamese, was bound to incite a spirit of revenge on the old French Empire textbooks. Mr. Phan was fond of quoting, with a short acerbic laugh, from the first words of the history he had had to memorize as a boy: *"Nos ancêtres, les Gaulois . . ."* In literature, Mr. Phan and I had had the same textbooks—Crouzet, Desgranges—but being an American I had no scars to show from the experience; it had not hurt my national pride.

Still, I was sorry to find that map on the blackboard. Beyond my personal disarray and regret at what appeared to me a kind of indigence (history was richer than those children knew), I was sensitive to the fact that at home this lesson would be regarded as sheer propaganda: "They indoctrinate the school children." Yet it was not ideological instruction they were receiving here, except for one set phrase, run together like a printer's slug—"The French colonialists aided by the American aggressors"—which had the merit of being factually true: Indochina in 1950 was a French colony, which was getting large quantities of military aid from the Americans, whose intentions were certainly not defensive so far as the Vietnamese were concerned. Rather, what the children were studying in the textbook and following on the map was a practical guide to action. This was a class in Preparedness. It would have been foolish, I guess, to expect to find them studying the Mongol invasions of the thirteenth century. They had probably had that in grade school, along with the history of the Two Sisters, Vietnamese Boadiceas, who had repelled the Chinese invader in the first century A.D. and ruled as queens until, defeated at the head of their army, they drowned themselves together in a river from grief.

In the next classroom we visited, they were having a lesson in solid geometry. The class rising from its desks was a trifle older, about seventeen, and there was only one girl member, somewhat plain. The boys were good-looking, some beautiful, even, with lustrous hair, shining eyes, soft clear skin—no acne in North Vietnam. The teacher at the blackboard, not much older than they, was very handsome himself, gay, laughing, kind. Most of these students, Mr. Phan thought, were the children of peasants; the teachers, who came from "away," lived in with the peasant families, as used to happen fifty or sixty years ago in rural America, when the schoolteacher boarded with farmers. Middle-class specialists from Hanoi were also housed with the local peasants, teaching them new farming methods: this province, formerly, had been backward. "Our experts have learned much from the people, too," Mrs. Chi, conscientious, appended. "It is a new experience for them." The need for learning from the people is often emphasized in the North; we have heard about that before, in the Soviet Union, where erring writers are sent to "learn from the people," as young delinquents in the capitalist world are sent to reform school. But on Mrs. Chi's lips the expression has a tender, Tolstoyan sound, a mild, soft, reverent note I have heard in the South, too, but there turning bitter or melancholy: the South Vietnamese on the U.S. side who care for the poor and the peasants—and there *were* some of these last year—despair of the American advisers' learning anything about the people, let alone from them.

In this classroom, I felt more comfortable. The conic sections on the blackboard were eternal, universal, democratic, the same in Hung Yen Province as in Tacoma, Washington. Here the class, when called on, unlike the history pupils, did not get the answer right on the first try; the problem was harder, requiring thought, not just memory of what was in the textbook. The teacher gently prompted and, seeing that his students were abashed before the visitors, quickly wrote the solution himself on the blackboard. I was invited to make a speech to the class. At the conclusion of a visit or tour, the guest is likely to be called on to sum up. "Now give us, please, your impressions of our factory/co-operative/school/dispensary." I was never any good at this and usually left it gratefully to my companion, but today I felt more confident. Having had that restorative impression of geometry as a binding universal, I wanted, in turn, to impress it on *them*. But either something went wrong with the translation or my thought, which was really propaganda for a disinterested world of pure forms, was too crazily tangential to their own interests or to what they were expecting to hear—anyway, whatever the reason, it fell flat. When the translator finished, the whole class looked bewildered, as if the words that had reached them had been an empty envelope that had traveled all the way from the U.S., airmail, special delivery, with no message inside.

Back at the province guesthouse, we ate a second meal under the parachute of the Drone they had shot down. At one end of the room was the wreckage of a bomber plane, which had lettered on it what appeared to be part of a name: "Lt. Ed. Van Or . . ." The Vice-President of the province (in the South he would be called the deputy province chief) was a former Viet Minh fighter: around his neck, he wore another trophy—a French jungle camouflage scarf. The cook, an old army cook resembling a sailor, had prepared a splendid carp—fished that afternoon from a pond nearby—with dill, tomatoes, rounds of carrots. The Vice-President poured little glassfuls of mandarin wine, a pink alcohol, very good, though sweetish, and many toasts were exchanged. As he drank the mandarin wine, under the leaking tent of the striped parachute (it was raining hard), his somewhat splayed features grew darker, his gold tooth glinted, and he made me think of that tough character Stenka Razin, the anarchist hero and brigand leader of the Russian marshes, who planted an egalitarian Cossack Republic along the whole length of the Volga in the time of Alexius—seventeenth century. (Does the reader feel that some of these comparisons are farfetched? They mostly come from my notebook and were taken down on the spot, hurriedly, lest I forget; for example, while Mrs. Chi, opposite, at our bedroom table in the guesthouse sat poring over the *Report of the Third Party Congress on Agricultural Matters.* A curious and maybe important thing about North Vietnam is just this historical resonance. Whatever seems strange and new there at the same time has an insistent familiarity: "Who or what does this suddenly remind me of?" Farfetched may be the right word.)

It was too muddy for the tour of a co-operative that had been scheduled. Instead, they showed us movies, and the Vice-President gave us many statistics about the province. He talked about the bombing, but there was not a great deal to tell; Hung Yen Province has not been heavily bombed—that was why it had been chosen for our visit. Only Xuan Duc, completely destroyed by 300 ordinary bombs; Minh Hai, badly damaged by phosphorus bombs; Lai Vu. He said American planes had dropped butterflies on the crops, which seemed strange: in the car, going home, Mr. Phan, for once erroneously, explained that he had meant insects—actually there is a bomb known as the butterfly. I asked if we could visit the province capital, which was only a mile or so off, but no, there was nothing to see there any more, they replied apologetically—just shut-up buildings; it had been totally evacuated.

Along the main roads of the North the visitor finds these ghost towns, ghost factories, ghost hospitals, suggestive of Death Valley, like the big still University of Hanoi. In Hoa Binh Province, the following week, we came one morning to a very large yellow modern building, with a number of outlying buildings behind it: Hoa Binh Hospital. It had been bombed on August 20, 1966. The roof of the main building—on which, our guides said, a red cross had been painted—was smashed in, and in the tall grass and weeds there were huge bomb craters. In the wilderness behind, the maternity pavilion was relatively undamaged; inside, patients' records were blowing about or lying scattered on the floor. We picked some of them up and examined them: mother, pyelitis; child, diarrhea, and so on. Along the main walk, ornamental plants were still growing, though choked by weeds. This desolate picture made one fear to ask the question "How many were killed?" "Nobody," our guides said, smiling. "But how is that possible?" "We had evacuated the hospital before the bombers came." They stood nodding. This was quite a usual thing. It had happened, for example, with the Thai Nguyen steel factory, the pride of the North. When the bombers came pounding, it was empty. Nobody home. Americans who dismiss talk of war crimes as "propaganda" would no doubt argue, if confronted with photographs, that the Hoa Binh Hospital might have been evacuated to serve as an arms depot. Possibly. Yet there were no signs of this, no evidence that the hospital had ever been occupied by anybody except medical staff and patients. The hospital looked as if it had been left in a hurry and as if nobody had come back since except bemused, head-shaking visitors like ourselves.

Such derelict structures would be pathetic, like forsaken hopes (the province hospital had been a new socialist achievement), if the story ended there. But, fantastically, a new crop of hospitals has replaced them, springing up in the fields and woods, sometimes under the protection of an overhanging cliff. A surgery is improvised in a grotto or in a thatched hut, with a generator run by kerosene and a tiny old frigidaire, kerosene-powered, too, stocked with serums and vaccines. The result of this migration of doctors and equipment may have been an actual improvement in public health: for instance, a highly trained young doctor from Hanoi has been "dispersed" to a traditional Thai community living in wooden houses on stilts. Clustering together in a valley, they look from a distance like natural elements of the wild landscape—a species of bird colony or apiary. We were received in one of those remote communities, still in some ways barbaric in its customs or savage in the old sense of the word. You take off your shoes before climbing up into the family dwelling; inside, there are two big central fireplaces, recalling the discovery of fire, one for the men to sit by, talking, the other for the women to cook over. There are mats and homespun coverlets on the floor for sleeping, the men at one end of the room, the women at the other. The women are chattering and heating food in iron pots under a smoke-blackened shelf where edible roots and ears of corn are drying; I am given a piece of fresh-roasted manioc—tapioca. Around the necks of the baby boys are silver collars or necklaces; the women wear earrings, and the young girls' breasts are bound, for reasons of modesty, in a tight, flattening bodice of hand-woven cotton. Yet thanks to the proximity of the evacuated hospital across a teetering log bridge, these primitive families have quickly learned hygiene: boiling their water, washing, making use of the new cement latrines. Their pigs, which used to live in refuse under the high-perched houses, are now installed in clean pigsties; these people are fond of pork. And the rapid evolution in folkways has been effected (credit must be given) by the "Johnsons" flying overhead and strewing a few bombs casually on another slumbrous Thai hamlet down the road a few miles, missing the hospital, if that was what they were looking for—there are no other "military" targets—in its shelter under a beetling crag.

"Out of this nettle danger we pick this flower safety" (Hotspur) could serve as Hanoi's motto in contemptuous answer to the Pentagon. Contempt for the adversary and for material obstacles and difficulties is the mood of the provinces, which now harbor most of the country's resources, like hidden talents:

dispersed industries, laboratories, medical staff, the young. Ho Chi Minh himself, according to rumor, is in a safe place in the country; that is why he has not been available to recent visitors to Hanoi. Imagination situates him in a cavern, like Frederick Barbarossa, waiting for his country's need to summon him back. In fact, on his return to what was then Indochina, in 1940, and again at the end of World War II, he *was* living in a cave beside a mountain brook, at Pac Bo, near the Chinese border. In the Museum of the Revolution, you are shown photographs of the cave, and his few simple possessions, relics of the hegira, are on exhibit, the most touching being his "suitcase," a small flat reed basket; he traveled light. With his many changes of name, which seem to signify so many protean incarnations, he is a legendary figure, a flitting place spirit or *genius loci*. The whole saga now being enacted of the dispersal bears his imprint: *mobility, simplicity, privation, resourcefulness.* The Vietnamese revolution has recovered its lyricism by returning to its primal myth of Ho's cave; the bombers furnished the inspiration.

Hoa Binh Province, to the west of Hanoi, is mountainous country, full of natural wonders and fantasies: caves, natural bridges, sugar-loaf peaks, weird stone formations resembling upright tombstones. The Black River winds through it, and it is not far from the Dien Bien Phu region, which, they say, has a similar geology and vegetation: the *ban* tree, linked with the memory of the Dien Bien Phu campaign, as much as the poppies of Flanders with World War I, grows in abundance on the mountain slopes. The first evidences of a Vietnamese culture of the Neolithic Age, about 5000 B.C., were discovered in the caves and grottoes of this province, when human remains known as

Hoa Binh Man were brought to light. Later remains, Bac Son Man, were found near Hanoi. Archaeological digs have not been halted by the war; in fact, they are part of the war effort, for the most recent Bronze Age finds are proving, at least to Vietnamese satisfaction, that already in the Bronze Age there existed a specific Vietnamese civilization having nothing to do with the contemporaneous Chinese civilization of the Han period —in short, that Vietnam, as an indissoluble entity, has always been and always will be.

A local official, introduced as the Permanent Member of the Administrative Committee, had come to meet us in the dark when our cars crossed the province border; he was an old resistance fighter from Quang Ngai Province, south of the parallel, plainly of peasant origin, with a kind, lined face and large genial-looking teeth. Through the woods, on foot, by the beam of a flashlight, he led us to an evacuated factory, which consisted of a series of workshops cleverly built under a cliff, a natural bombproof shelter. This was remarkable enough, but he was saving a surprise for us: a chamber or "room" in the mountain, closed on four sides except for a man-made portal; here Hoa Binh Man's descendants were manufacturing farm machinery. Some boys had found the cavern, lowering themselves into it from a small aperture in the top, through which now you could see a few stars; the people had blasted an entrance with dynamite, and an electric cable had been run in from the generator below. The night shift was at work (the factory ran continuously, on three eight-hour shifts), almost all of them young people, including some Muong girls from another "ethnic" tribe of these mountains wearing their tribal earrings and bracelets and shy as birds of strangers. In the glow of a forge, under the natural vaulting, it was an operatic scene, which Verdi might have scored, with a chorus of revolutionary patriots; I thought of *Ernani*. As in the factory in Hanoi, where the young girls had been making generators by hand, the work in this secret chamber was *artisanal*, handicraft applied to turning out labor-saving machinery, *e.g.*, a power tea-roller for extracting the juice from the leaves.

In the woods, not far from the workshops, was the wreckage of a U.S. plane; they took us to see this artifact of an Aluminum Age civilization, directing shafts of light on it from their screened flashlights to find its number and make: somewhere nearby was the pilot's grave. Again I thought of *Ernani* and the night scene at the tomb of Charles V. Verdi's *risorgimento* music, his love of storms, night, patriots, freedom fighters, is well suited to the North Vietnamese theme of struggle. On our return to Hanoi, two nights later, we passed a crowd assembling at the entrance to a large grotto in the mountainside; it was Saturday night, and the country people were going to the movies in an "evacuated" movie house.

Hoa Binh Province, though considered relatively safe, had been bombed more often than Hung Yen Province. There was some bombing while we were there, and one morning we saw a flight of Air Force planes pass over on the way from Thailand, but they did not bother with our little procession of cars. The bomb damage in this region disclosed no pattern of attack: here the hospital, there some houses for workers from a sugar plantation, here a small repair shop for farm trucks, there huts and fields, here an agricultural school (March 4, 1966, forty rockets, twenty fragmentation bombs; one worker killed in the school laboratory, laboratory destroyed, three teachers injured). Out the car window I glimpsed a stone bridge collapsed over a stream. "Air Force?" Mr. Phan, with a big smile, shook his head. "*We* did it. In our war against the French." I would never have known the difference, of course, but Mr. Phan was a proud stickler for accuracy; he did not want any mistakes in my notebook. Along a short stretch of the road on which we were driving, Route 6, 4,000 CBU (anti-personnel) bombs had been dropped last year.

The danger was made vivid by the miles of trenches surrounding the reconstructed agricultural school, now spread out over a wide area in camouflaged huts in which were installed classrooms, dormitories, a refectory. You had to wade through a stream to reach the school or approach it more adventurously from another direction by motorboat or sampan—they would not let me do this. The narrow straw-lined tunnel trenches, like mole runs, with points of entry every few feet, were supposed to be particularly effective against CBUs. This underground network extended for three and a half miles. Every morning boys and girls coming to school across the fields toted their bundles of possessions with them and deposited them in neat piles at the tunnel outlet nearest their classroom: homespun coverlets, sleeping mats, zipper bags—everything they owned. This was in case their strawy dormitories caught fire from a raid in their absence. Yet despite the danger and the hardship, perhaps even because of it, spirits in the school were high. Classes were being held outdoors, under the trees, in a pre-holiday atmosphere resembling that of a small American college in June, when seminars are gathered under an oak or an elm. On a table moved out into the sunlight, a makeshift chemistry laboratory was set up for an experiment; the students, who were going to be agricultural technicians, were getting a foundation in the sciences. A school chorus entertained us with songs. Our pictures were taken. But their lunch was waiting on the refectory tables: rice, a hot stew, vegetables. We left.

Some of the teachers walked with us as far as the stream we had to ford. I remarked on the evident, glowing health of the students. A woman teacher agreed. "The life outdoors is good for them." She sighed a little, shaking her head. I do not know what shadow was crossing her mind. Possibly she was reflecting on the mystery of good coming out of evil or—a related thought —on what would happen afterward, when the bombers went away once and for all. Would this pastoral scene be dismantled, as helmets were put away, camouflage leaves brushed off, city children returned to their parents? I frequently wondered, myself, especially in such idyllic circumstances, how the population would react when the spur of the bombing was removed. There would be no further need for factories hidden in the mountains, disguised schoolhouses strung along the fields and woods, tunnel networks. Could all that art and artifice be institutionalized— photographed and stored in museums?

But possibly the teacher was thinking of something quite different: the front. While we stood by the stream exchanging formal good-byes, at Khe Sanh the Americans would be totting up the morning's North Vietnamese body count. That subject is never mentioned in the North, at least not when company is present. Being human, they must talk about it among themselves.

Yet hearing no allusion to battle casualties (though they do not
deny, except officially, having troops fighting in the South), you
actually forget that the sons, husbands, fiancés, brothers, cousins
of the cordial people you meet are being killed in a certain
proportion every day. It was only when I left North Vietnam
and opened a capitalist newspaper that I was reminded, with a
start, of the North Vietnamese dead. I asked myself how for
two and a half weeks, with young soldiers everywhere, training
or marching, I could have let that slip my mind. The power of
persuasion, no doubt. The North Vietnamese, confident of the
immortality of their nation, of its powers of dispersal and
subterfuge, had infected me with their sense of superiority to
the daily facts of death.

A subsidiary explanation might be that there were no re-
minders present—no wounded limping or being lifted, white and
bloody, into a helicopter, such as I had seen in the South, no
field hospitals, no corpses packed up for shipping as at the
airport at Phu Bai. The North Vietnamese soldiery was dying
elsewhere. Out of sight, out of mind, then? Yet quite often in
the North, I remembered our Marines at Khe Sanh, and only
the night before, in the hostel where we were staying, the Permanent Member, a good man, I thought, had been talking of that
hell with pity and horror for the young Americans trapped in
it; the older North Vietnamese, especially men who had been
in combat themselves during the earlier war, would sometimes
reveal an earnest, unfeigned sympathy for the American ground
soldier—a sympathy they did not extend to the pilots taking
off from their comfortable, secure bases in Thailand or on the
carriers of the Seventh Fleet to release their bomb loads on the

population and return home for supper. So what was happening just south of the parallel must have been in the minds of all.

When the North Vietnamese maintain silence about their losses —to the wonderment of the foreign press, no over-all statistics are furnished even on the domestic casualties inflicted by the U.S. bombers and the guns of the fleet—it cannot be that there is an official conspiracy to conceal the truth from the population. The Voice of America and the BBC are not jammed, and, so far as I know, there is no ban on listening to them. The official silence must rest on a general consent: "We do not discuss our losses." No wonder the foreign guest does not seek to know, does not let his mind stray in that direction. I asked what was the name of the little stream we were about to wade through. The school principal scratched his head; he interrogated the teachers. "It seems it does not have a name," Mrs. Chi translated. "There are so many streams here; they cannot give names to them all." Everybody burst out laughing, as though the idea of fixing a name, like a ticket, to a minor natural occurrence resembling countless others was a bizarre American notion. And they were laughing, too, surely, at the prompt resourcefulness of their answer: how a seeming poverty—lack of a name— was turned into a proof of inexhaustible wealth—streams so abundant that speech could not find words for them.

Language

Communication was no problem with the North Vietnamese. Though only a few interpreters spoke English, some officials read it, and everybody I met of middle-class origin over the age of forty—ministers, poets, critics, museum workers, doctors, specialists in information, the head of the Supreme Court— spoke French fluently. Even those who had no second language, a factory manager, for instance, were remarkably well informed about the United States. Coming from the West, eagerly bearing news of American political developments, we found they knew it all already: the New Hampshire primary, the dollar crisis, the latest editorial in the *Wall Street Journal*. Nor were they dependent on "peace" sources; I kept seeing old copies of *U. S. News & World Report*. They were familiar with the voting records of Congressmen whose names I had barely heard of. The head of the Writers' Union referred to Noam Chomsky's work in linguistics and helped me out while I was groping for the author of *"Nihil humanum mihi alienum puto"*—Terence. You did not have to explain to them what a primary election was, a just-about-hopeless job with French political intellectuals, or sit squirming as I had done recently at a Paris press conference on the draft-resistance movement while speakers invoked "Samuel Bellow" and "William Thoreau." The events that happened during my stay in Hanoi—the reassignment of Westmoreland and Admiral Sharp, Johnson's March 31 speech, the

73

Wisconsin primary, the murder of Martin Luther King—were instantly known in the Thong Nhat Hotel; I heard Johnson, live, on the Voice of America, and our friends from the Peace Committee came to tell us, with a delicate sympathy—"Perhaps it may not be true"—of the death of King. As I established when I got home (my husband had saved the French and American and English papers), no important happening in the West had missed us in Hanoi or been distorted in the reporting. The only gap was in news from the East: Poland and Czechoslovakia.

Yet there *was* a difficulty in the sphere of communication—a sort of speech impediment. Though we talked of the same things, we did not always use the same language. Take "Viet Cong." This name, which started out as a derogatory, derisive label, like "Commie" a few years ago in the United States, has passed into popular currency in the Western world, becoming the normal straightforward term for the insurgent forces in the South. If the term were taken away, nobody in Saigon could write a newspaper dispatch. In the South last year it had no pejorative sound, any more than "Gothic," originally injurious, for a cathedral. The derogatory word was "Charlie": "We caught Charlie with his pants down," "Charlie is hurting bad." By contrast, the abbreviation "VC" was a half-affectionate diminutive, like "G.I." But in the North, as I quickly perceived, the term "Viet Cong" was impermissible, since "Cong" was short for Communist, which was what they insistently denied about the leadership and inspiration of the movement. The right expression was "the People's Liberation Army."

I could not use it. For one thing, it was too long. For another, it was too heavily sloganized, like our "Free World Forces" to describe the Australians and Koreans in the South, which I could never use either, not if they gave me the water torture while a U.S. soldier watched. Maybe it is a literary prejudice to dislike such words as "free" and "people" when what they refer to is uncertain. When Johnson talks about "the American people," he means the supporters of his war policy, and when the North Vietnamese talk about "the American people," as against "the Johnson clique," they mean the opposite. Are the American people the majority or the workers or the peace movement or who? Perhaps they are a Platonic Idea.

On the other hand, I found it perfectly natural to say "the Front" or "the NLF," meaning the political entity. The National Liberation Front was its name, and one does not argue about the names of political parties and organizations. Such names, by common consent, have turned into simple signs, and only a sinister demagogue like Senator Joe McCarthy, who made a point of talking about "the Democrat party," instead of the Democratic party, will try to smudge them. But a political entity is abstract, unlike guerrilla fighters in Ho Chi Minh sandals and black pajamas. For me, "the VC" is the human and evocative term. Finally, on my tongue "the People's Liberation Army" would have been horribly hypocritical, considering how often last year on the other side of the parallel I had been saying "Viet Cong" and "VC." One cannot use language as a sort of reversible raincoat, wearing the side out that is best suited to the political climate where one happens to be at the time.

This "block" gave rise to problems, which in retrospect have their amusing aspect, I being the embarrassed comedian doing the splits. In the North, people were curious to hear about my experiences in the South, particularly the Southerners by origin, some of whom, trustful of the Geneva Accords, had left their families behind in 1954, like Mr. Ngo Dien, of the Foreign Ministry, whose seventy-six-year-old mother was living in a village somewhere south of Saigon—he still hoped to see her before she died. The separation of families, assumed at the time to be temporary, is one source of the bitter sense of betrayal felt in the North and directed toward Diem and his memory as well as toward the Americans. When the men of the Viet Minh went north, they counted on the elections, promised for 1956, to reunify the country; they also counted on postal service between the two halves, which Diem abolished. The theme of separation plays a great part in the war literature of the North, and two little volumes, *Letters from South Vietnam*, have been translated into English: these letters, mostly from women, reached their addressees, the reader is told, through diverse channels; wife writes to husband, sister to sister, daughter to mother. And even if they may have been considerably edited to suit the popular taste ("My darling, Today is the happiest day in my life. That is why I must write to you. I have just been appointed to the leading committee of self-defense groups in our village!"), the popular taste is there, and reading them, as the Preface explains, will give comfort to the many families without news. Of course I had no news of a family kind to tell, or of guerrilla defense units either, but I could name off the towns and villages I had visited, and even those former Southerners who had left no close relations behind wanted to hear about their native places. "What is it really like in Saigon now?" "When you were in Hue, did you go to see the Emperors' Tombs?"

The last question, simple enough to answer, you would think, led immediately into difficult terrain. "I saw one." "Only one?" "Yes. Americans weren't supposed to go there. They said the tombs were full of Viet Cong. But a young German took me one Sunday in a Red Cross station wagon to visit Tu Duc's tomb; it was very peaceful actually. Only ordinary people from Hue walking around the little lake with parasols. It was sad; the little pools on the terraces were covered with green scum. But we didn't try to go to the more remote ones, which I guess really were in VC territory." Such sentences, I found, were possible because very light, almost invisible quotation marks were placed, as if by agreement, around the words "Viet Cong" and "VC." Implied was a faint dramatic irony, which permitted the listeners to smile indulgently, as though hearing a disembodied voice coming from AID or JUSPAO. Similarly with "What is the attitude of the students in Saigon University?" "They don't like the Americans but, being middle-class, they're terrified of the Viet Cong. As your President Ho Chi Minh said once, speaking of students and intellectuals, it is a confused milieu." Laughter. Or "In Saigon, everyone is nervous, looking over his shoulder. They say, for instance, that all the pedicab drivers are VC." No doubt the North Vietnamese, who are intelligent, perceived my discomfort. Perhaps they would have found it ludicrous to hear: "The tombs are full of People's Liberation Army cadres." Or "The pedicab drivers are all militants of the People's Liberation Army." Or perhaps not.

Those hovering quotation marks were a convenient traffic device for circumventing obstacles, and I sometimes had the impression that the Vietnamese with whom I was talking, especially when they were men of my own age or older, rather enjoyed the rapid navigation around enemy words and expressions. And it is not clear to me, looking back, whether the quotation marks were put there weakly by me or whether they sprang up all by themselves. Sometimes a sudden hesitation or gulp, as when, not looking where I was going, I arrived at "Viet Cong" big as life in a sentence and could find no way around it, produced that effect of framing or distancing—an alienation effect.

A worse problem was "the war of destruction," for here there was no question of light humor. But I was averse to using those words to describe the thing; to my ears they sounded like one agglutinated word, stuck together once and for all so that you could not unstick it. If emotive phrases are wanted, I prefer to put them together myself—bourgeois individualism. Yet to avoid the expression involved painful circumlocution when the simple word "bombing" would not fit the case; I would have to falter out something like "The bombing and shelling of your country which began in February 1965 and is still going on," as we chatted in the shelter waiting for the All Clear. Still less could I say "the U.S. imperialists," "the U.S. imperialist aggressors," or "the neo-colonialists." My word was "We."

Quite early, and with violence, I resolved that never, no matter what, would I hear myself reciting "the puppet government," "the puppet troops" when called on to speak of the Thieu-Ky government and the Arvin. It was no better in French. *"Le gouvernement fantoche." "Les fantoches."* Nor could I explain why that word led all the rest on my aversion list, especially in the mouth of a Westerner; I did not mind it so much when the Vietnamese said it, except that it made reply awkward. When somebody has been talking steadily about "the puppet government," you cannot chime in with "the South Vietnamese government," since their point is that Thieu and Ky are not a legitimate government, but American tools. The same with the army. My solution was to talk of "the Saigon government" and "the Arvin." Yet why all the inward fuss about that word? It could not be mere American touchiness. I do not care for the word "satellite" when applied to the Eastern countries of the Soviet bloc. Perhaps it is because men, even if they do not fight very well and are corrupt and steal chickens, are not puppets; a puppet is made of cloth. It is quite possible to say or write "The Saigon government is a puppet of the United States." Agreed. But to reiterate the notion every hour on the hour, far from making it truer, awakens the critical spirit: for a puppet, Ky, for instance, has been quite a handful. A figure of speech, overworked, takes its revenge by coming to life, and you wonder who is the puppet, the Arvin soldier or the orator who does not tire of calling him that, mechanically, like a recording.

Yet the North Vietnamese attach great importance to this formula. You can read in the daily English news bulletin published in Hanoi a dispatch from Reuters or UP: "The South Vietnamese [puppet, Ed.] government met this afternoon to discuss a draft of eighteen-year-olds." Conversely, when a U.S. agency quotes Radio Hanoi, you read: "The puppet [South Vietnamese government, Ed.] forces suffered heavy losses today at Bien Hoa." At that point, it becomes a war of words on both sides, a fight between blue pencils conducting search-and-destroy operations on a daily basis.

One awkwardness for a Western writer in a Communist country is that he is committed to a convention of freshness, of making it new. In antiquity, originality was not so highly valued, and it has occurred to me that the set phrases of North Vietnamese diction are really Homeric epithets. Compare "the insolent wooers," "the long-haired Achaeans," "cloud-gathering Zeus," "the hateful Furies" with "the American aggressors," "the American imperialists," "the war of destruction," "the air pirates." And no doubt, too, they are Oriental ideograms; some, like the "just cause," are the same in the South as in the North, though with different referents, of course. There is also a prescribed, quite angry Marxist language in the Eastern European countries, but behind the Iron Curtain, as opposed to the Bamboo, it is not a *spoken* language; the *Izvestia* correspondent in the Thong Nhat Hotel used the ordinary vernacular when he drew up a chair to our table, like party members in Warsaw, Cracow, Budapest, but probably when he wrote for his paper he used the official language, just as a man in the Middle Ages wrote in Latin and spoke in the vulgar tongue.

Anyway, it has to be acknowledged that in capitalist society, with its herds of hippies, originality has become a sort of fringe benefit, a *mere* convention, with accepted obsolescence, the Beatnik model being turned in for the Hippie model, as though strangely obedient to capitalist laws of marketing. Not only that; the writer's "craft" is more machine-tooled today than the poor scribe likes to think. How could he compose without his apparatus of dictionaries, thesauruses of synonyms and antonyms, atlases, glossaries, Fowler, Follett, to direct him to the right word? In prose our industrial revolution dates back to the Flaubert process, invented about 1850, which can be roughly defined as the avoidance of verbal repetition: except for emphasis, do not use a word (excluding prepositions, pronouns, articles, and connectives) that you have already used a few pages back; find another, *i.e.*, a synonym. Application of this unnatural process is now all but automatic with us—second nature. This may be because we keep on describing the same old things—that is, bourgeois society—and some stylistic variation is needed or everyone would die of boredom. A magazine like *The New Yorker* is especially nervous about the repetition of words and phrases; underscoring and marginal question marks call the contributor's attention to the fact that an adjective he has used ("employed"??) on galley 3 reappears on galley 8. Similarly, a phobic dread of clichés is manifest in the jittery styling of *Time*, whose whole editorial policy is to reduce people and events to filler and boiler plate.

Nevertheless, an American is what he is, and a writer perhaps more than most, in that he has to stick close to his language, listening to what it will let him say, and it will not let him talk in ready-made phrases except in jest or mockery—mockery of authority and the sacrosanct. The American language is self-conscious, like a young person. Hence the cat sometimes got my tongue during long car rides with my friends of the Peace Committee, and when we conversed I tried to bypass subjects that would oblige me to say "the Americans" or "We" while they were saying "the neo-colonialists" or "the Johnson-McNamara clique."

Instead, I asked them about the flora and fauna of the regions through which we were driving. In that way, I learned something about the native trees, flowers, birds, folk remedies, how the rice seedlings were transplanted, the difference between Vietnamese tea and Chinese tea. Like the geometry lesson on the blackboard in the school in Hung Yen Province, botany and zoology re-assured me with the promise that they would be there when the war was over and the last "Johnson" had been shot down from the skies. My companions probably thought me quite a strange person—superficial—and indeed I felt myself that to be so concerned about the names of flowers and trees (the dragon's eye—*Nephelium longanum*; the early-flowering bridal *ban* tree, slightly reminiscent of the New England shadbush; the red-flowered kapok, the abrasin—an oleaginous tree whose product is used to polish airplane parts and gun bores) was a luxury typical of a capitalist author, who could afford the pedantry of nomenclature, just as if North Vietnam were still Tonkin (another unmentionable word, of colonialist memory, like Annam, which made it tricky to discuss the Tonkin Bay inci-dent), and Frenchmen in tropical helmets were still exploring the upper reaches of the Mekong, looking for the shortest route to China, while Englishmen were writing in the Britannica (eleventh edition): "In the wooded regions of the mountains, the tiger, elephant, and panther are found, and wild buffalo, deer and monkeys are common. The delta is the home of ducks and other aquatic birds. Tea, cardamon and mulberry grow wild. . . . The natives are skilled at enamelling and the chasing and ornamentation of gold and other metals." If only that were all, but the unnamed ethnographer had more to contribute: "The Annamese (see ANNAM) is of somewhat better physique than those of the rest of Indo-China. . . . (ANNAM) . . . The Annamese is the worst-built and ugliest of all the Indo-Chinese who belong to the Mongolian race. He is scarcely of middle height and is shorter and less vigorous than his neighbors . . . his hair is black, coarse, and long; his skin is thick, his forehead low. . . . Though fond of ease the Annamese are more industrious than the neighboring peoples. They show much outward respect for superiors and parents, but they are insincere and incapable of deep emotion." The old Britannica would not be spared if we white people began our cultural revolution; that doubtless whiskery Edwardian who looked on the "natives" as zoological specimens was a cultured ancestor of the G.I.'s who cut "Charlie's" ears off as souvenirs—it was just a fad, they say. But the tea, the cardamon, and the mulberry? Must the mind be forbidden to collect them in its neo-colonialist trunk?

Luckily Mr. Phan shared my (let me still hope) harmless interest in the names and properties of things in Nature, and he was always happy to acquire an English word, "seedling," for instance, in exchange for a Vietnamese word, and to chide me when I kept saying "betel," when I ought to be saying "areca." "The *betel leaf*," he wrote firmly in my notebook, and "the *areca nut*." The point is that the betel leaf, which comes from a pepper plant, is chewed together with the areca nut, which comes from a palm. Or *used* to be chewed. In the North that bad habit (betel acts like a drug or intoxicant) has practically disappeared; to my surprise, only once or twice did I see the blackened teeth and gums so familiar in the South. Mr. Phan confirmed my observation. Small, sturdy, dark-skinned, with a wide, confiding grin ("They say I am a Stokely Carmichael"), chain-smoking, in a brown leather jacket, he was something of an explorer himself. We compared travel notes. He knew China, Russia, Poland, Cuba, where he had stayed at the Havana Hilton. He showed me a short piece he had written in English about a trip he had taken last summer through his own country in which he had carefully set down the good points and the bad of what he had seen. He gave me "the Vietnamese man-of-letters recipe for making tea": the pot must be scalded, and the water be just below the boiling point—first the bubbles coming to the surface will be the size of a crab's eye; wait till they are the size of a fish's eye, then pour over the tea leaves. Mr. Phan was a harbinger and a bustler and often prepared our "visits." His great ambition was to visit France.

Clearly in these conversations, while searching for common ground, I was trying to hold onto my identity—a matter of loyalty, refusing to betray oneself. But this could be read two ways. In that very refusal was I not betraying myself in the unpleasant sense of showing my true colors? Having been an anti-Stalinist ever since the Moscow Trials, I had remained, I thought, a socialist of a utopian kind. In North Vietnam, the vocabulary repelled me precisely by its familiarity. I had heard that jargon before, and too many lies had been told in it: "the people's democracies." Yet *were* they all lies? I suddenly recalled the comfortable American joshing of U.S. officials in Europe a few years back: "You old capitalist warmonger, you!"

Ha ha. But if not true at the time, let us say up to 1960, it was already in the process of becoming true, prophetically, as those decent, amiable men were confidently laughing it off. The Bay of Pigs was waiting in the wings. And from the Vietnamese point of view—a point of view which I must say I gave little thought to until it was too late, *i.e.*, until 1964—the United States had been capitalist-warmongering at the side of the French practically since the death of Roosevelt and right up through Dien Bien Phu. And the current term "the American imperialist aggressors," like it or not, expressed the current truth. Whatever the motives, originally, behind the U.S. intervention in Vietnam, at present there was no doubt that it had turned, as if by itself, perhaps with nobody in particular propelling it, into a war of aggression, and capital investments were waiting to follow the flag, personified at a low level by the would-be real-estate developers piloting airplanes I had met in the South and at a high level by Mr. Lilienthal and his Mekong Valley development project.

As for the air war against the North, it was certainly a war of destruction and not of interdiction, which was at first pretended, unless the two terms are synonymous; you could "interdict" the flow of men and supplies to the South by destroying all life in the North, a program, I hear, that is within the technical capacity of the U.S. but is not contemplated because of the damage foreseen to the American "image."

What the United States calls propaganda is in fact reiteration. Our officials, like our writers, want to "make it new." Give us a little variety, the U.S. delegates at the Paris conference and their echoes, American newsmen, moan after the North Vietnamese delegates have said, once again, that all acts of war against the Democratic Republic of Vietnam must cease. Meanwhile, U.S. policy, unvarying in content, has been clothed in seasonal changes of words as the years have rolled by. Johnson "limits" the bombing by announcement March 31 while actually intensifying it; his speech writers design new wardrobes for the steely corpus of his Baltimore address, which reappears in Manila, San Antonio, Washington, thickly disguised in woolly presidential "offers," which seem to blind the American electorate but not the Vietnamese, who have no difficulty seeing through to the old naked proposition: reciprocity.

It is reiteration that even sympathetic Americans find wearisome in the North. "Are they still harping on that leper colony?" an American said to me when I mentioned the subject in the Thong Nhat Hotel; he had heard all about it last year, on an earlier visit, and his attitude was that they ought to change the phonograph record. "Well, actually I *asked* them about it," I replied, defensive. "I'm interested in lepers because of the ones I saw in the South." He accepted the excuse, but there was no doubt that he felt that the North Vietnamese were over-exposing their cause. As though they could use some lessons in public relations, the soft sell.

Yet, to be fair, it was natural to get bored and impatient sometimes when obliged to listen to what you already knew—otherwise, why would you be here? Tangible facts never bored me, facts of destruction and counterfacts of growth, nor did real exchanges of ideas or snatches of autobiography, but it was different with formal speeches, feature films, documentaries, plays, playlets, songs, poems, lithographs, oil paintings, which were all implacably about war and defiance. The documentaries were fairly interesting in themselves, educational (though at home a little of martial bee culture might have gone a long way), and the feature film they showed us was superior to most Hollywood war movies, yet after the third or fourth private screening, it was understandable for a Westerner (especially one who is not very fond of movies) to suffer a loss of affect and then immediately feel ashamed, to look around, for instance, restlessly in a projection room during a sentimental sequence—the heroine was leaving her father to risk her life standing guard over a delayed-action bomb—and find a Vietnamese girl silently weeping in the next seat.

They are moved by their films, by their graphics, by the endless photographs and mementos in the Museum of the Revolution. They delight in the animated relief model of Dien Bien Phu displayed in another museum whose name I forget—a panoramic history of the battle with little trucks and troops moving, cannon firing, lights winking on and off, which in fact was delightful and extremely ingenious, like the electronic *crèche* I had seen in Sicily last winter with the Magi arriving on camels and shepherds grazing their sheep around the Eiffel Tower, the Colosseum, the Taj Mahal, and the Empire State Building. Pop devotional art, combining the reverent and the playful; people's art for once in the real sense.

Some of the weariness I felt was unselfish. If I longed for a change of theme, that was partly for my companions' sake, for the whole Vietnamese population. But the North Vietnamese cannot get enough of this material, which to them is, quite simply, true to life. If a magic carpet were to transport them to a performance of *Don Giovanni,* they might find it false and tedious. The girl who was crying at the movie had been telling me, apropos the pellet bombs we had seen in the War Crimes Museum, about one of her friends, a schoolteacher, who had been walking along a country road with a pupil when the planes came; she flattened herself out to cover the child and was lucky —she got the pellets only in her back. Next year that story, sufficiently commonplace in the North to command universal belief, could be turned into a movie with newsreel shots of real bomber planes. As they explained to us matter-of-factly in the Hanoi feature-film studio, they had plenty of footage of bombers; such shots did not have to be faked. In the U.S., scenes of the "air pirates" attacking schoolteachers and children would be dismissed as crude "propaganda." "I'm allergic to propaganda," an American newscaster said to me after a showing of some North Vietnamese documentaries, with the air of one owning up, proudly, to an idiosyncrasy, a national mole or case of freckles. Did he mean he liked his news dry or *brut,* without any addition of feeling? In the war art of all kinds I saw in North Vietnam there was nothing that to *me* was recognizable as untrue.

One-sided, you might argue, except that in my opinion the Americans do not *have* a side in this war, that is, do not have an excuse, surely not that of ignorance. This war is no *Antigone,* where both Antigone and her uncle Creon are right according to their lights. No *Iliad* either. Furthermore, the Americans as shown in North Vietnamese feature films and animated cartoons are not so much villains as merry caricatures; they are meant to be laughed at, like the French colonialists, who, in their day, were satirized in witty colored prints. Nor are they only targets for humor. At the Writers' Union, a young writer described the plan of his new novel: to present in alternate chapters two points of view, that of a simple G.I. and that of a North Vietnamese soldier—both would be sympathetic. No doubt somewhat wooden also, but that is not the point. At the War Crimes Commission, Colonel Ha Van Lau, a delicate-featured, slender, refined officer from Hue, of mandarin ancestry (he reminded me strongly of Prince Andrei in *War and Peace*) discussed the problem of conscience for the U.S. pilots; some, he thought, were aware of what they were doing and some were naïve or deceived. The pilots in North Vietnamese hands are brought to repent (if in reality they genuinely do) not by being fed lies or, in my judgment, mysterious drugs, but by a simpler method: shortly after their capture, or as soon as they are able, they are taken to see some bomb sites—the first step, it is hoped, in their reformation.

What you see on the stage, in films, and in street posters is not untrue or viciously biased, unless you think that rubble of a school, church, hospital, TB sanatorium is biased. On the screen and in graphics, you are shown heroes and heroines, but the Pentagon itself would not deny that the North Vietnamese people are heroic, though "tough" would be the word preferred. Even if the figures of planes shot down are exaggerated (and I have no way of testing this), their defense of their land has the quality of an epic, *i.e.*, of a work of art surpassing the dimensions of realism. Seen in movie terms, it is a thriller, a cowboys-and-Indians story, in which the Indians, for once, are repelling the cowboys, instead of the other way around. No normal person, set down in a North Vietnamese rice field beside an anti-aircraft unit manned by excited boys and girls, could help being thrilled, whereas in the South, beside an artillery battery, surrounded by sandbags, you share the sullen gloom of the population and the sardonic resentment of the soldiers.

Nevertheless, the Westerner in North Vietnam, stirred and convinced by the real thing, finally resists its aggressions in art and falls back on some Wordsworthian preference for emotion recollected in tranquillity. Besides, hortatory art has the troubling property of resembling all other hortatory art, which makes it difficult to distinguish, for instance, fascist architecture from Stalinist architecture or socialist realist painting from Roman Catholic oleographs. In the visual field, North Vietnam is no exception to this rule; the declamatory painting and sculpture seem to be reliving, phylogenetically, the history not just of socialist realism but of allied species including U.S. post-office murals and paintings of Pope John. A war monument in Hanoi is interchangeable with, stylistically, the war monument in Saigon, and neither has any relation to Vietnamese tradition, which in the North survives only in folk art—charming decalcomania-like designs of fish, birds, roosters, who exceptionally have not been recruited to the war effort.

Obviously, in a short official stay in North Vietnam, I was not in a position to meet dissenters, if they existed. But I was able to use my eyes and when feeling bored during long speeches in Vietnamese, film showings, protracted visits, I could look around me, seeking a fellow-sufferer. Boredom is one of the hardest of human emotions to conceal, and the Vietnamese are the reverse of inscrutable (though they sometimes leave you to guess the cause of the lively emotions that are passing across their faces), yet it only happened twice that I noticed a sign of flagging interest except in myself. Every member of the audience was following what was said or shown with evident absorption and approval.

The exceptions stand out. One was in the Hanoi feature-film studio, where a young director was openly, obdurately bored while his chief was talking. Artistic "temperament"? Hostility to U.S. intellectuals, regarded scornfully as tourists? The other was during a visit to an anti-aircraft unit in Hanoi when the blushing young political commissar of the battery read aloud an especially long speech of welcome he had evidently written out that morning, with great pains, in a round schoolboyish script. It was the day the bombing stopped north of the 20th parallel—April 1, Hanoi date. Glancing over the boy's shoulder, the lieutenant of the outfit, a somewhat older man, ascertained after fifteen minutes or so that he still had two closely spaced pages to go (a point I had been checking on myself from the other side of the table) and kindly but firmly indicated that the speech should draw to a close. "That's enough," is what he said, in Vietnamese. Everybody smiled broadly, with grateful relief, and perhaps especially the boy, as he folded up the sheets of paper and tucked them back in his pocket.

Not only were there no signs of disaffection; the announcement, on March 21, of a decree against "counter-revolutionary crimes" took even long-resident foreign journalists by surprise. Nobody could understand what or whom was aimed at. The list of fifteen counter-revolutionary crimes punishable by jail or death comprised treason, espionage, plotting, armed rebellion, sabotage, defecting to the enemy, disrupting public order, making propaganda, intruding into the territory of the DRVN. The last perhaps offered a clue. These activities, after all, must already have been very illegal, as most of them are in any country, but just then a U.S. invasion was being discussed as a serious or semi-serious possibility in the American press. Was the Hanoi government warning future collaborators of the punishment that would certainly follow? But who *were* those future collaborators, unheard and unseen until this moment and now produced like a photo negative by the law formulated *against* them?

Perhaps they were a mere apprehension in the mind of Hanoi. What was striking here in comparison to other Communist states was the utter, total absence in conversation, movies, plays, pictures, short stories, of the theme of treason. Not a word about backsliding, incorrigible elements, "former" people. The figure of the "wrecker" or evil counselor never cast his shadow. There was no question of any villain or faint heart opposing the war; at most, there could be a problem of priorities, whether, as in a play they took us to, it was more important for a young medical student to continue his studies at the university or go to the front. Mr. Phan decided that two acts were enough, so we never saw the end, but it was clear that the hesitant student would finally choose action over inaction: he was basically a "good" boy.

"Former" people must exist in North Vietnamese society but the only evidence of this I had came from Saigon ("My uncle in Hanoi," said a lady, "used to own eighty houses; now he has only one"). In Hanoi I did not hear of that uncle or anyone like him. "What has happened to the landowners?" I asked once. "The ones who didn't go south?" "If they agree to work with us, we accept them," was the reply. "We do not hold their past against them." The subject did not seem to be of much interest. If an ex-landowner were to appear in a film script, he would be already reformed. No, there is another possibility: he might undergo a conversion from "former" to present, bad to good, as he saw the bombs falling on the irrigation project, the dikes, the sweet-potato field—a perfectly plausible story which no doubt could be documented by many real-life examples.

Conversion, from bad to good, or vice versa, which was the great theme of Western nineteenth-century fiction and of early movies, is never represented in Western novels these days and seldom on the screen. It is as though the West had agreed that people were incapable of change. You do not see Bonnie and Clyde *decide* to become mass murderers; no choice seems to be offered them. In the Free World, to judge by its artifacts, nobody is free to make a decision to be different from what he is. But in the un-Free World, the opposite is assumed, and one indication of revisionist tendencies in a Communist country is the gradual disappearance of regenerative themes in popular art. By this criterion, Hanoi, unlike Belgrade, Prague, Budapest, even Moscow, is a bastion of anti-revisionism.

Nor is this found only in movies and plays. While Novotny, say, in Czechoslovakia has been given up as a bad job, the North Vietnamese still have hopes of converting even their worst enemies. The idea of forgiveness and rehabilitation is underlined by North Vietnamese and NLF officials in discussing the government functionaries of the South. "Anyone who wishes to come over to us is welcome." Once, in a conversation with Ngo

Dien, the small, gentle, slightly mournful Press Chief of the Foreign Ministry (the one whose mother is in the South), the topic came up, and I, half teasing, tried to test him, choosing the most horrendous example: "What about Ky?" "Even Nguyen Cao Ky," he said, gravely nodding his head up and down while at the same time smiling at the enormity of the thought.

Whether Nguyen Cao Ky would have to do penance—and how much—is another matter. What I am trying to describe is a state of mind I found in the North, at once categorical and in a strange way indulgent. People say of Communists that they see everything in black and white, which is certainly true of the North Vietnamese rhetoric: "bandits" engage in "dark maneuvers" with the aid of "pen hirelings." But beneath the forbidding rhetoric there is something else. Unlike Western liberals, they do not accept difference, but they accept change axiomatically as a revolutionary possibility in human conduct—which Western liberals do not; that is why liberals have to be tolerant of difference, resigned to it.

The North Vietnamese reiteration of their "correct position" implies the conviction that their enemies, if they hear it stated often enough, will understand; it is so *clear*, they seem to be saying. "Johnson," officials repeated, "can call off the bombing *in five minutes* and have talks. Why not, then?" This was said with genuine mystification, in the plaintive hope of getting an answer to a puzzle. Johnson was pursuing a mistaken policy; even the stock market was telling him so. Why *not* correct it? Far more than his American critics, the North Vietnamese officials put themselves in the President's place. They spoke of offering him "an honorable exit," an idea repugnant to *me*. Their questions, in short, rested on the proposition that Johnson was free, like any other human being, to change his course. The opposite is pretended and possibly believed by Johnson, who acts like the honest prisoner of circumstances, locked into a bombing policy that now bears the name of "a first step in unilateral de-escalation." In the Stalinist days, we used to detest a vocabulary that had to be read in terms of antonyms—"volunteers," denoting conscripts, "democracy," tyranny, and so on. Insensibly, in Vietnam, starting with the little word "advisers," we have adopted this slippery Aesopian language ourselves, whereas the North Vietnamese, in their stiff phraseology, persist in speaking quite plainly; the term "regroupees" (infiltrators, Ed.), mainly accurate at the outset to describe North Vietnamese forces fighting in the South, has quietly been withdrawn from the dialogue. Although we complain of the monotony, the truth, renamed by us "propaganda," has shifted to the other side.

First Principles

One morning early in our stay, they took us to visit the Hanoi University Surgical Hospital—pale-yellow pavilions in the French colonial style set around an older central building in landscaped grounds. It was known as the German-Vietnamese Friendship Hospital because funds to rebuild and enlarge it had been given by the East German government. In the South, the Medical School at Hue University had been set up by the Adenauer government, with a staff of West German doctors: challenge and response. In the Hanoi hospital, there were no German doctors. The staff was Vietnamese. The chief surgeon and head of the hospital had been trained in Hanoi under the French; he had formed his first surgical team in the forest during the Resistance War, operating sometimes forty-eight hours at a stretch. Twenty years later, Professor Ton That Tung was still forming surgical teams, but his work schedule had dropped to eight hours a day; he had younger doctors under him, qualified nurses, laboratories, asepsis.

When they had dressed us in sterile gowns, we were admitted into the operating rooms, which contained the latest thing in equipment and instruments, gauges of all kinds, sterilizers, tanks, looking very much like home, despite the fact that some of it was of Chinese and Soviet make; the pride of the hospital, though, seemed to be equipment from England. They had no emergency cases that morning; the doctors had long finished operating, and there was the usual mid-morning lull of a big well-run hospital.

The wards were clean and tranquil, though the walls could have stood some paint and the sheets were grayish, possibly from the lack of a "magic ingredient" in the washing powders used; I thought of those old ads showing a shamefaced house-wife and her Monday wash on the line and the words "tattle-tale gray." They said they had found that sheets lasted longer than the traditional mats. The white iron beds were adjustable, and each had a mosquito net and pillow. The floors were swept; patients in fresh hospital jackets were reading quietly; some had vases of flowers. Many were receiving intravenous drip injec-tions. Charts were clipped at the foot of each bed. It was the "slow season" for bomb victims, they told us, because of the monsoon; most of the patients were ordinary surgical cases. No surgical hospital can be anything but grim, but conditions here, including the state of the bedding, compared favorably with what I had seen in the surgery ward of a big Parisian public hospital.

They showed us photographs of the old hospital, as it had been in the French times: half-naked patients two or three to a bed (in one ward some were lying, semi-animate, on the floor), no mosquito nets, no bedding, general misery and squalor. "But that's exactly what I saw last year in the South!" I said ex-citedly, and Dr. Ton That Tung, plump, pink, pleasant, with horn-rimmed glasses and white hair in a kind of bob, fell back a pace, his jaw dropping. "No!" "There were no patients on the floors," I emended. "But two to a bed, yes. And people said there were often three."

He shook his head several times, incredulous. He came from Hue, of royal stock, he had just been telling us, and like many Southerners I met in the North had an automatic reaction of dis-belief when "filled in" by a foreigner about his native place. Perhaps he had been assuming that the NLF stories he had heard were propaganda. In the North, I found, they cannot really imagine the South as it is today, above all the refugee camps; they have no experience to match it. And contrary to what their enemies might think, the men of Hanoi do not enjoy hearing about disease, suffering, degradation, in the U.S.-held areas of the South. Like Dr. Ton That Tung, they change the subject.

With American intellectuals, far from the scene, it is dif-ferent; they are shocked but content to be shocked, in that it proves their point: they are *right* to oppose the war. What all this shows, no doubt, is that Americans need reassurance in their opposition to Johnson's Vietnam policy, while the Viet-namese don't. For the middle generation, a doubt persists, just as it did for veteran Marxists at the time of the Moscow Trials; a Trotskyite friend once confided that he used to wake up at night sweating: "What if Stalin is right?" Thus the terrible news of the slave-labor camps was welcomed by us, as confirma-tion, while the news of the Nazi death camps was received at first with stunned disbelief, the difference being that we were certain Hitler was evil and shrank, quite humanly, from further proof of it—the correctness of our judgment was not in question. Not that the fear of being wrong politically is an undesirable quality per se; only, when it starts feeding on human suffering to fortify an *argument*, it is time to watch out. This happens on both sides of the Great Debate on Vietnam. Nobody could pretend that the U.S. negotiators in Paris were *sorry* about Viet Cong rocket attacks on Saigon. If Tocqueville was right, and we are a nation of lawyers, it would explain a good deal.

Leading us rapidly through the hospital garden, with a glance at the slightly overcast sky (there was no alert that morning), Dr. Tung showed us the underground operating room. If necessary, he operated in the shelter, but he did not like to do so, because of the damp and the mold. Pointing at a fungus stain on the ceiling, he made an angry grimace. In his office, he discussed the extraction of bomb pellets from the brain, passing around photographs and X rays of a woman teacher and a young boy. Often the best course was to leave the pellet and remove the splinters, which cause abscessing. He indicated the tiny entry hole in the woman's thick hair; without an X ray machine available, it was sometimes impossible to find where the little steel balls had penetrated the skull; in such cases, the patient usually died. He showed us X rays of patients with pellets in the chest, to illustrate the zigzagging path the pellet described, in contrast to the ordinary gunshot. As he held the X rays up to the light, in his short-sleeved white gown with vigorous forearms bared, he seemed a "pure" professor of surgery lecturing on the interesting problems presented by these novel projectiles. All the cases he was describing had recovered; he brought out another series of photographs showing them walking in the hospital grounds. "I took a special interest in that boy," he interjected, pointing to a youth of about fifteen—a complicated chest case with multiple wounds.

Extraordinary that so many recovered, someone said. Dr.

Tung nodded. Most bombing victims—from cluster bombs or normal explosive bombs—could be saved if they were operated on promptly, within six hours at most. Speed, they had discovered, was of the greatest importance. In the case of multiple wounds, he would have three teams operating simultaneously on the patient. And he applied oxygen inhalers throughout the operation—a new technique they had learned in the war. I asked him about anesthetics. Most socialist countries, he said, used local anesthetics, but he preferred sodium pentothal. But the kind of anesthetic was secondary. The main thing was to make sure that the bomb victim was given injections of plasma or a saline solution—against shock—as soon as he reached a doctor or a medical technician. Plasma was not always available, and his surgical teams had found, to their surprise, that it did not matter greatly what you injected; the point was to inject it. Even water would do. I thought I had not heard right. He smiled. Yes. Plain water. The question of finding a cure for the coma induced by pellet bombs was of great popular interest, I learned later. In the play they took us to see, a young doctor, the wavering hero's mentor and influence for the good, has gone to the front—i.e., the DMZ—to work on such a cure in the laboratory of the battlefield.

It was typical of the North Vietnamese to hit on a curative element, water, so basic that medical research had overlooked it up till now. Like the purloined letter hiding where everybody could see it. A return to first principles (which signifies to *the people*) gives them much delight, especially when it can also demonstrate the exercise of ingenuity. Such a first principle is bamboo. I had the impression that the North Vietnamese were

103

almost pleased when a metal bridge was bombed, so that they could get together and make a pontoon bridge, lashed into place with bamboo; still more, one of those folding bamboo bridges, taken up in the morning and hidden all day from the straining "round" eyes overhead, to be swiftly replaced at nightfall, when the supply trucks start to roll. The resources of bamboo make it a folk-tale trickster. "Look!" said Mr. Phan, pointing to the electric-power poles strung along the highway in Hung Yen Province. "Yes. Rural electrification," I said, missing the point. "Bamboo!" he exclaimed, laughing. "In this province there is not much wood!"

For fractures, Hanoi-trained surgeons have been trying a system of bamboo splints used in folk medicine. The aerial war and the dispersion have given an impetus to the scientific study of folk or, as they call it, traditional medicine, side by side with advanced Western techniques—an idea long favored by the Minister of Health, Dr. Thach, French-trained, and of royal blood also, a cousin of the deposed Bao Dai. In his mountain dispensary, a young surgeon, Dr. Tung's pupil, has a frigidaire stocked with serums for operations and a cupboard stocked with jars of traditional remedies for snake bite, rheumatism, and other local ills. It is reasonable that tribesmen living for centuries in a snake-infested region should have found successful antidotes, but what about a plant juice that experiment has shown to be astonishingly effective when injected against bomb coma? And according to Mr. Phan, an old wives' poultice made of a live young chicken pounded into a paste, laughed at for generations by city people, has proved to be a remarkable healing agent for war wounds.

In his office, Dr. Tung talked of folk medicine. As a Vietnamese he was excited by the idea of progress through deliberate and controlled regression, *i.e.*, by rediscovery. On his desk was a Champa head of a woman (ninth to eleventh century, southern Annam), of a style rather similar to the Khmer style; reproductions of this head are quite common—she is the North Vietnamese Nefertiti. Like French doctors with a good practice, he was interested in art and archaeology. As a present, he gave me a pretty bronze arrowhead of the Chou dynasty (classical Bronze Age), and a volume of Vietnamese poetry rendered into French; some of the translations were by him. In return, I sent him Konrad Lorenz's *On Aggression*, which I had been reading; he was aware of Lorenz's scientific work.

On the floor were a number of large cartons containing surgical and medical supplies waiting to be opened; they had arrived that morning from a London committee for medical aid to North Vietnam. He took us to the hospital library, which had shelves lined with medical classics in a variety of languages, mainly Western, and stacks of recent publications from France, England, Germany, America. He kept up with professional developments in the United States. He remembered American surgeons he had met at conventions and found their names and addresses in his notebook. "Before the war of destruction," he said, his field had been liver transplants, which he had successfully performed on animals; he was following with interest American results in human beings.

He showed us the laboratories, with a slight air of apology. After the war, they would build a new hospital, maybe, with more modern facilities and better experimental equipment. Now the medical school, hospitals, and laboratories were nearly all dispersed to the provinces. Most bomb victims were treated at the district level; only the more complicated cases were sent to Hanoi. It was not possible, in any event, to expand a research center when a bomb could destroy it tomorrow. American doctors, I remarked, to cheer him up, were too dependent on the laboratory. They were losing the gift of diagnosis. Soon they would not be able to spot a case of measles without the help of a computer. He nodded. The present sickness of the world, in his view, was the result of a lag in adjustment to technology. It was odd that the same thought had been expressed to me long ago on a beach on Cape Cod by a Hungarian psychoanalyst, who estimated that it would take mankind two centuries to recover from the effects of the Industrial Revolution. Dr. Tung sighed. "Neolithic man with a bomb in his hand." Here in Vietnam the problem was not acute, fortunately. "I operate with my ten fingers." He held out his "surgeon's hands"—with the characteristic broad palm and long slender fingers—and looked at them, smiling, as at a set of favorite tools. Surgery, ultimately, was a tactile matter. Touch—the second sense. "Of course sometimes I use instruments," he added. "But they are not essential. In the forest we did not always have instruments."

Last year at Saigon University, I told him, there had been much agitation for giving medical instruction in Vietnamese; I had heard a lot of debate about it. Here there was no debate, he said. Instruction was given in Vietnamese. But what about the vocabulary, I asked. To me, it had seemed a clumsy and (though I did not say so) chauvinistic proceeding to create a medical terminology in a minority language that did not have the words for it, especially when a majority language—French —was already implanted in the country. What would happen to a young doctor with a strictly Vietnamese medical vocabulary who was invited to attend a congress in Bordeaux, for instance? And how could he keep up with the medical literature?

Dr. Tung recognized the objections. *"Oui, madame."* But the decision to teach in Vietnamese had not been a matter of choice. Language, after all, was the key to medical understanding, and the new state had needed to form a corps of doctors fast, drawing on the peasantry as well as on what remained of the former privileged classes. It would have taken too long to train medical students if you had had to teach them French first. Of course, they had been right, I had to admit, and righter than they could have known at the time: when the Air Force came, a medical corps was waiting for it.

The practical wisdom of the decision, if it required demonstration, was evident when you thought of the South (750 doctors last year for a population of sixteen million and most of those serving in the Army), where civilian casualties were infinitely more numerous and where the presence of foreign medical teams, a drop in the bucket in any case, aggravated xenophobia in the native medical personnel, leading to petty feuds, theft of AID supplies, and actual obstruction. In the North, a single province, Hung Yen, now has fifty doctors and 800 assistant doctors for a population of 670,000 (one doctor and four nurses in 1954). The North, moreover, has kept its independence from its allies, in medicine as in the military sphere. No foreign doctors are serving in the country (no Russians, no Chinese); though aid is accepted, it remains in Vietnamese hands. Even in pharmaceuticals, they have aimed, when possible, at self-sufficiency. Against tuberculosis, they have found a vaccine that differs from the Western type in that it uses dead bacilli instead of live ones. For the Sabin vaccine against polio, which requires refrigeration and hence is unsuited to local conditions, they have substituted a similar vaccine of their own invention that will keep for a month at normal temperatures.

It had not been too difficult, Dr. Tung said, to create a Vietnamese medical vocabulary. They had based themselves on the Chinese, which had all the terms they needed. Here his own French training was a handicap; he was still learning the new Vietnamese words. Inwardly I blushed. I had forgotten about Chinese medicine. It was perhaps not such a deprivation that Dr. Tung's pupils would be unable to make themselves understood at medical congresses in Bordeaux or Montpellier. Or even New York. What would send them there? They would be meeting colleagues in Moscow or Peking, which should not be a reason for grief. Just the same, I found it slightly disquieting to see that the professor's young white-gowned, white-capped associates, though they nodded and beamed, could not follow a word we were saying. It was like that with the young people everywhere in the North: doctors, factory engineers, army men, film-makers, the whole new intelligentsia, a few literary men excepted. I felt sorry for the French language, which was dying out in a country where it had lived so long—extinct or extirpated, like the passenger pigeon. My conservationist instincts protested. In another twenty years, who would be able to read the medical texts in the hospital library?

To regret the passing of French was to regret the passing of the cosmopolitan old order, "the language of diplomacy," and so on. But it was also to regret those fluent old revolutionaries pentecostally blessed, like the Apostles, with the gift of tongues —Lenin, Trotsky, Ho Chi Minh, and behind them Rosa Luxemburg, Marx, Bakunin, and our own Benjamin Franklin, who sits like a funny antique in the garden of the American Embassy in Paris. Among the young, all over the world, the coming Western language is English, and North Vietnam is not an exception, though held back by a shortage of teachers. English has a demonstrable utility, which gives both a socialist incentive and an excuse for learning it, just as being an interpreter or a professional translator excuses an American or a Russian for having a second language in the eyes of his monolingual compatriots—it is OK if he has to do it for a living. But this narrow view of my own language distressed me, liking frills and "useless" knowledge for myself and everyone else. I was sorry to see young people in North Vietnam discard French, when they had it, in order to push forward with English. On the other hand, the eagerness to learn and practice English showed an amazing lack of chauvinism. Young militants from the peace movement arriving in the North had even created a preference for *American* English over the language of the BBC—an entering wedge perhaps for a whole range of U.S. folkways, appetites, and habits. Or would Americanization, a creeping disease, stop with Joan Baez, Bob Dylan, and protest songs?

Visitors from the peace movement were not the only teachers. When I was allowed to see two captured pilots in the living room of a Hanoi villa (I am not sure whether this was their actual place of confinement), it was clear that the North Viet-

namese officer present was following the general drift of the
conversation, not having to wait for the interpreter to determine
if I was transgressing the boundaries of the questions I had
been asked to submit in advance. In fact, I did transgress them
in the nervous give-and-take of the talk (we quickly exhausted
"Health," "Family," "Treatment," "Current View of the
War"), but the officer indicated that it was all right to go ahead
eliciting such facts as that a pilot was raising carp in a pond and
learning to play chess with his fellow-prisoners, that he would
have voted for Goldwater if he had been registered in 1964
("because the Army was for Goldwater"), that when peace came
he would like to get out of the Army and teach math and coach
athletics in a high school. Before the interview, I had been told
not to mention Johnson's speech, which we heard that morning
(April 1, Hanoi time) but which the North Vietnamese people
had not yet been informed of. I did not mention it, but one of
the pilots did: "I know Johnson has said that he isn't going to
run again." "Where did you hear that?" I exclaimed, startled.
"I read it in a UP report." I glanced at the Vietnamese officer,
but he merely smiled and let the conversation continue. "I see
you know English," I said to him at one point. He shrugged.
"A little." But the guards, who were younger, were not shy of
showing off the words and expressions they had been picking up
from their prisoners. A strange sort of cultural exchange,
largely one-way, for though one pilot told me he had read "a
lot" of Vietnamese history in jail, he seemed wholly unmodified
by his experience, and the sole question he put me was "Can
you tell me how the Chicago Cubs are doing?" The second
prisoner, an older man, had not changed his cultural spots

either, except in one respect: he claimed to like Vietnamese candy.

The Vietnamese, one hears, have been taken aback by the low mental attainments of the pilots, who have officer rank (the gaunt, squirrel-faced older man led in to see me was a lieutenant colonel) and usually college degrees, which must be leading their captors to wonder about American university education. I was taken aback myself by a stiffness of phraseology and naïve rote-thinking, childish, like the handwriting on the envelopes the Vietnamese officer emptied from a sack for me to mail on my return for other captive pilots (the regular mail from North Vietnam is slow), printed or in round laboriously joined cursive letters. If these men had been robotized, I felt, it had been an insensible process starting in grade school and finished off by the Army, which had passed them for duty as high-precision instruments, equipped with survival kits and the rudiments of reading and writing. Far from being an élite or members of an "establishment," they were somewhat pathetic cases of mental malnutrition. Quite a few American visitors shrink from interviewing the pilots, and before I went, acquaintances in the hotel (including our guides) expressed sympathy: it would be painful to meet one's own countrymen in such circumstances. Avoid questions of guilt and conscience was the general advice. It *was* painful, because of the distance between being free and being under duress, between leaning forward on a comfortable sofa and sitting upright on a stool, but also because of another, unexpected distance—not a moral one, for I did not feel morally superior to those American strangers in prison pajamas, if anything the reverse, since they were "paying" and I wasn't,

111

but a cultural distance so wide that I could see myself reflected in their puzzled, somewhat frightened eyes as a foreigner. As between co-nationals, this distance itself was a crime against humanity, a reason for protest, for revolutions; not that the pilots felt it so, probably infinitely preferring being themselves to being me, whom they almost certainly regarded as a tool of the North Vietnamese Communists, a tool shaped by Eastern education, money, advantages. And if they thought that, they were right in a sense, for to be against the Vietnamese war was an economic privilege enjoyed chiefly by the middle and professional classes. It was largely owing to privilege that I could feel more at home talking French with Dr. Ton That Tung, say, on medical and philosophical subjects than making lame conversation in English with those wary cagey pilots about hobbies, church, family, and the American primary elections.

As it happened, the men I felt most immediately at home with in the North were all from Annam (now renamed Central Vietnam, which makes it sound like a featureless administrative unit): Dr. Tung, Pham Van Dong, Colonel Ha Van Lau of the War Crimes Commission, and the fatherly "Permanent Member" in Hoa Binh Province, although, being of peasant origin, he spoke only Vietnamese. Ho Chi Minh came from Annam, too, of a minor mandarin family; many revolutionaries were formed there, in the shadow of the Emperor's court, and went to school together at Hue University. The Annamites are not well liked by the other Vietnamese, or so I was told in the South. They are the Tuscans of the country, while the people of Tonkin are the Milanese, and the Cochin Chinese are the Neapolitans or Sicilians. Annam, like Tuscany, is looked upon by its

112

neighbors as a basket of crabs—difficult, self-sufficient, proud, provincial, obstinately "local," frugal, tradition-bound, vain of its past.

But these qualities, mostly rural and conservative, are in fact typical of the whole North Vietnamese style of making a new world, embodied in Mr. Phan's "Personally I hate anything artificial," in the tenderness of the intelligentsia for the peasantry and for what the Florentines call the *popolo minuto* (barbers, tailors, small craftsmen), in the sense Hanoi, like Florence, gives of being a large village, where the notables take the air in the evening on the main street. For example, on the night of April 3, when Hanoi gave its answer to Johnson, on coming home from the theater, we found standing in front of the hotel a group consisting of the Minister of Health with his daughter, the small, informally dressed Chief Justice of the Supreme Court, and Colonel Ha Van Lau. They had probably been attending some "friendly dinner" in the hotel (the North Vietnamese expression for an intimate banquet) and had lingered on the sidewalk chatting. When they saw us, they waited to hear what we Americans thought of Hanoi's answer, which was handed to us in mimeograph by a smiling and excited Mr. Phan, and were frankly pleased by the verdict: *"Très intelligent."*

The feeling that Vietnam is a close community or family is sometimes quite strong in Hanoi, as when our guides of the Peace Committee appeared all dressed up in their best suits one afternoon because we were going to visit the National Liberation Front and that was like visiting your most important relations. "We always wear our best clothes when we visit them," they

113

explained, as my companion rushed upstairs to change out of his corduroys. "To do them honor because they are in the front lines and we are in the rear." And at the NLF Delegation, as if to mark the shade of distinction, we were given dressed-up party refreshments: a chocolate liqueur and oranges instead of the usual tea or beer and bananas. Everybody in the North seemed to remember, with irony, General Nguyen Cao Ky, the black sheep of the family. An official in the Foreign Ministry dryly recalled him enrolled in a band of school children at an Independence Day celebration, waving his little bouquet and noisily chanting: "No one loves Ho Chi Minh more than the children!" That is the sort of performance one's relations, cruelly, never forget.

I began to wonder what role the Lao Dong Party played in this network of relationships. "May I ask, what proportion of you in the hospital are Party members?" I said to Dr. Ton That Tung. He burst into loud laughter. They had never counted, he said. Party membership had no significance here. I could see that the question had given offense, which was mystifying since in other socialist countries I knew—Poland and Hungary— curiosity on this subject was treated as normal, and anybody was glad to tell you who was a member of the Party and who wasn't, just as a matter of interest. In fact, though fond of describing himself as a "Communist"—"I am of royal blood and a Communist!" was a joke he repeated at our farewell "friendly dinner"—Dr. Ton That Tung, as I heard later, was not a Party member, and there was no secret about it. Then how had my question been indiscreet? When I told the story to a foreign diplomat, he was puzzled. It was true, he said, that Party membership did not play much of a role here, in comparison with other Communist countries. But maybe just for that reason it was looked on as a private matter, of no concern to outsiders. In any case, the words "Role of Lao Dong Party?" remained blankly in my notebook. I did not want to risk offending again.

For me, the local ethos was clearest in the figure of Pham Van Dong, who received us on a Sunday morning on the front stoop of the presidential palace (formerly the residence of the French governor general), wearing a freshly ironed North Vietnamese army jacket of gray-tan poplin with unbuttoned flap pockets and a collar that showed his still-youthful throat. In the middle of the conference table in the room where our talk took place was a little bunch of roses and carnations from the palace gardens, and when we stood up at last to leave, he slowly picked out a few blooms for each of us, as I have seen an old-lady horticultur-alist do in New England, carefully matching the posy to the char-acter of the receiver, so that you guessed you were having your fortune told in the language of flowers and would have given more than a penny to know what the flowers were saying. Ho Chi Minh used to have the gallant habit of saying it with a single rose to women correspondents; Nora Beloff of *The Observer* remembers the red rose he chose for her at the Fontainebleau Conference. Such courtly manners have an element of impulsive theater, which is not to say that they are rehearsed.

Pham Van Dong is a man of magnetic allure, thin, with deep-set brilliant eyes, crisp short electric gray hair, full rueful lips drawn tight over the teeth. The passion and directness of his delivery matched something fiery, but also melancholy, in those coaly eyes. An emotional, impressionable man, I thought, and

115

at the same time highly intellectual. He had an odd grave mannerism of repeating the final word in a sentence, as though savoring it on his tongue, especially when it had a bitter taste. *"J'ai été roulé, roulé,"* he said, speaking of Geneva, meaning that he had been "stung" like a countryman at a horse fair. During our conversation, which lasted two hours, he used none of the prevailing political clichés and did not waste time on long preambles recapitulating facts or arguments already known to all parties. He came at once to the point. When he intended to evade a question, he made that almost teasingly plain, as when I asked him about the counter-revolutionary laws just promulgated—why now? "Till now, being a new state, we have been very busy," he said. "We have just got around to putting those laws on the statute books." As happens with frank people, he inspired openness in his questioner. Had I thought of it that morning, I could have asked him, for instance, about the Lao Dong Party. Unfortunately, his general lack of hesitation in speaking his mind put most of our talk off the record. In the driveway, as we were leaving, he took account of his indiscretions and asked us, with slight concern, not to repeat certain remarks. Later I got a message passed through his secretary reminding me of four points—really four and a half —that it would be better not to mention. The reader need not fear he is missing state secrets, only the kind of thing we all say and hope will not "get back" to third parties, by which I do not mean Russia or China; neither was referred to that morning. In fact, Russia and China were never at any time referred to in my presence in the North except as distant occurrences in geography, history, art, cuisine.

During the conversation, an aide came in to whisper that there was a pre-alert. "If you don't mind," the Prime Minister said, "we will stay here in my office." I did not mind at all; indeed I felt honored to be included in a contempt for danger so strong and evident that it made me feel safe. To this fastidious man, I thought, bombs were a low-grade intrusion into the political scene, which he conceived, like the ancients, as a vast proscenium. Besides, it was unlikely that "we" would strike the presidential palace at this juncture; in twenty-four hours, Johnson's voice would be heard from the White House, putting an end to the raids on Hanoi. . . . Impossible, of course, to have known that, yet, looking back, I am sure we all sensed that day, had been sensing for a week, that some change was coming, although that evening, as if to deceive our radar, there were three real alerts in quick succession, about ten minutes apart, which sent us to the shelter for the last times.

That morning, with Pham Van Dong, we talked about *l'après-guerre*, whether it would be possible in peacetime for North Vietnam to pursue the original socialist path the war had opened. This—not negotiations, a formality; not an atomic war, which he brushed aside—was the great item on the agenda of the Vietnamese people. Foreign observers interested in varieties of socialism had been quick to notice on trips about the countryside the effects of geographical decentralization on the political structure. More autonomy on the province and district levels and more worker participation in the decisions of factories and co-operatives. What would happen afterward? Pham Van Dong, as I now realize, was perhaps not wholly pleased by the attention enthusiastic foreigners were turning on the phenomenon. This

117

is a touchy area in the whole socialist world. It is a question how much decentralization, *i.e.*, democratization, a Marxist economy can permit itself without regression to capitalist modes. The Yugoslav model of worker management is denounced by orthodox Marxist-Leninists as a sly return to bourgeois practices: competition, the need to show a profit, even advertising. Nor is it certain that the conservatives are wrong in their suspicion that direct democracy—village and factory councils—will "inevitably" lead to anarchy, in the pejorative sense of chaos, or, if not, to a market economy unpleasantly resembling capitalism.

To see North Vietnam as the scene of such an experiment is not an altogether entrancing prospect for the leadership. What if the enemy, capitalism, repulsed by air and foiled by land in the sister South, should creep in the back way, insinuating itself into the very organs of the people's rule: provincial and district committees, factory and co-operative directorates? Then all the sacrifices of the war would have been in vain—a point missed by libertarian well-wishers eager for further change. Yet the progress made in decentralization under the spur of the war offers a challenge to continue in that direction, counting precisely on the nation's spirit of sacrifice and self-discipline. There is also the old tradition of hamlet self-government, summed up in the saying, frequently repeated by foreigners, "The Emperor's rule stops at the hamlet gate," or—a variant— "at the bamboo hedge."

Hanoi listens to these urgings and declines to commit itself. Ever since the judicial murders and popular uprisings of 1956, resulting from the harsh agrarian reform laws, Vietnamese

118

socialist planning has been based on an idea of limit. This is the originality, emphasized by Pham Van Dong, of the Vietnamese "way." By refusing outside help in the form of troops, they have succeeded in limiting the war. Fearful of a population explosion, they have limited births (they are experimenting with a plant juice formerly brewed by witches in the "ethnic" regions and which appears to work something like the Pill); thanks to the bombing, they have been able to reverse modern demographic trends and actually reduce the population of cities. New institutions are introduced with care. For instance, hamlet cemeteries, to replace the family grave mounds in the rice fields. "What do you do with the old graves?" I inquired in a rural co-operative. "Dig them up?" The co-operative chief reacted with horror. "Do you think we want a *revolution?*"

The worship of ancestors, less a superstition than a veneration of the past, must not be disturbed; despite the difficulties the old graves make for modern farm machinery plowing and harrowing around them, only the newly dead go to the cemetery. No cultural revolution would be thinkable here, since culture—the accretion of the past—is the guarantor of Vietnamese independence. The delicate position of Pham Van Dong's government is that it is bent on preserving Vietnamese traditions but it is also bent on preserving the sacred tradition of socialism, *i.e.*, watchful central planning. On the one hand, it proceeds with an almost tactile sense (cf. Dr. Tung's surgical fingers) of what its people—and their history—will accept or reject. On the other, it insists on what is "good" for them; this is a moral, ascetic government, concerned above all with the *quality* of Vietnamese life.

Material scarcity is regarded as a piece of good luck. Fortune was kind when she made Vietnam poor except in skills. I said something anxious about industrialization. To Pham Van Dong, this was a joke. "We are an agricultural nation." "But you keep hearing about 'the industrial North.'" He shook his head and laughed. They made a little steel. "We don't need much heavy industry. That is not a problem for us. Light industry. Workshops." What he seemed to have in mind was a sort of bicycle socialism, as if here, too, there should be a limit, and the bicycle would be a good place to stop. He spoke of our automobile-TV culture as of something distastefully gross and heavy; Vietnamese ethics are permeated with ideas of lightness and swift pliability: bamboo, bicycles, sandals, straw. As though society's burden of goods should be no heavier than what a man can carry on his back. With a full-lipped contempt very like the contempt he showed for danger, he rejected the notion of a socialist consumer society.

At the time, the implications of this were not clear to me; I was only conscious of a feeling of happy agreement, remembering the ominous meeting between Mr. Khrushchev and Mr. Nixon in the model kitchen, like a domestic spat in the infra-red setting of some future One Hell from which nobody could escape except possibly to a trailer camp. But it now comes to me that in those words, with that fastidious grimace, he may have been vetoing the very program I had just told him was "dear to my heart": further decentralization for North Vietnam. In Vietnam I perceived—what doubtless I should have known before—that the fear of decentralization and local autonomy evinced by Communist leaders is not necessarily an abject solicitude for their own continuance in power; it is also a fear of human nature as found in their countrymen, on the assumption that modern man is "naturally" a capitalist accumulator, already spotted with that first sin in his mother's womb and ceaselessly beset by marketing temptations: if you let workers run the factories, they will soon be manufacturing Cadillacs because "the consumer wants them."

Yet the Prime Minister may have been implying the reverse: his faith that the Vietnamese people could assume a greater say in production without abating their idealism. The wares of modern consumer society as displayed in the South might well serve as a deterrent for their Northern brothers, like some dreadful emetic mixed with alcohol to cure forever a taste for drinking. The samples of U.S. technology that had been showered on the North were mainly in bomb form, yet the ordinary Vietnamese was able to make a connection that eludes many American intellectuals between the spray of pellets from the "mother" bomb and the candy hurled at children in the South by friendly G.I.'s, between the pellets and *all* the Saran-wrapped products of American industrial society which can no longer (at least this is my conclusion) be separated into beneficial and deleterious, "good" and "bad," but have become homogenized, so that "good"—free elections, say—is high speed blended with commercial TV, opinion-testing, buttons, streamers, stickers, canned speech-writing, instant campaign biographies, till no issues are finally discernible, having been broken down and distributed in tiny particles throughout the suspended solution, and you wonder whether the purpose of having elections is not simply to market TV time, convention-hall space, hotel suites, campaign buttons, and so on, and to give employment to commentators and pollsters. Since nobody can live in a vacuum, nobody, whatever he thinks, is free to "drop out"; poor blacks rioting carry home whiskey and TV sets.

To the North Vietnamese—and this applies equally to peasant and Prime Minister; "We are a mature people," they are fond of saying—American life appears not just grotesque, but backward, primitive, pitiably undeveloped, probably because of its quality of infantile dependency. A story, surely true, is told in Hanoi of a shot-down pilot who explained to his captors that his sister in the States was a rich *"industrielle,"* she would pay them for chicken and whiskey, if they would let him have them, and if they would let him go, she would pay an indemnity for any personal or property damage he had caused on his missions —he swore it: "My sister's a millionaire!" With such flying models being deposited on their territory, like beings from an archaic world, Pham Van Dong might trust at least the present generation to be immune to capitalist temptations which elsewhere seem an inherent danger of revisionist adventures.

It was Luu Quy Ky of the Journalists' Union who told us the sad story of the greedy pilot, early in our stay; the day before we left, at a farewell meeting, he announced that he was going to sum up for us the characteristics of the Vietnamese people. Here they are:

1. *Amour de la patrie.* Love of fatherland.

2. *Esprit laborieux.* Industriousness.

3. *Esprit de solidarité et entre-aide mutuelle.* Spirit of solidarity and mutual aid.

4. *Subtilité et persévérance.* Subtlety and perseverance.

5. *Optimisme. Esprit rieur.* Optimism. Gaiety and merriment.

6. *Esprit internationaliste. Pas de chauvinisme.* International-mindedness. No chauvinism.

I spoke earlier about undergoing an identity crisis in the North. This was due no doubt partly to the bombing, which "shook me up," but also to an unspoken feeling of conflict with the North Vietnamese value system, a conflict that grew more and more obscure as I sought to bring it to the light. Some vague assurance of superiority, not personal but generic, had been with me when I arrived; it was the confidence of the American who knows himself to be fair-minded, able to see both sides, disinterested, objective, etc., as compared to the single-minded people he is about to visit. To be just to myself and to those who brought me up, I think I do possess those qualities, though perhaps not as much as I imagine. They are the fossil remains of the old America, detached by an ocean from the quarrels of Europe, having no colonial interests compared to the Great Powers, a permanent outsider and hence fitted to judge or bear witness, enjoying a high material standard of living, which ought to exclude any venality or pettiness. That is how the heroes and heroines of Henry James saw themselves and how their author saw them, with amazed pity and terror. Even after World War II, the words "I am an *American citizen,*" pronounced by a New England spinster, could strike fear into the heart of an UNRRA official, as though the old green passport carried full investigative powers into the management of international relief funds.

My own avowed purpose in going to the North was to judge, compare, and report back; my findings, I reasoned, could not be damaging to the North Vietnamese but, on the contrary, by making them real to the reader, might dispel some of the phobic attitudes that were allowing the war to continue. A sound, sensible purpose, which I have not lost sight of, but which took for granted my supreme authority as an American to determine the truth. I counted on the public to believe me, as it had believed Harrison Salisbury, when all earlier reports had been discounted, as coming from suspicious sources. Yet after a few days with those single-minded North Vietnamese, I found my claim to being a disinterested party starting not exactly to disappear, but to shrink from showing itself, as if ashamed. The Vietnamese, beginning with peasants eagerly showing you where their fields had been bombed, had an earnest, disarming conviction that you would give them total credence. To question facts, figures, catch small discrepancies would be to abuse this open, naïve (from a Western point of view) trust. The same with their certainty of victory, which soon you began to share, to the point at least of hoping they were not wrong and blotting from your mind as disloyal to their struggle any information leading to a different conclusion that you had been reading in the Western press. But more unsettling than this quickening of sympathy—inevitable, humanly speaking, under the circumstances—was a sense that my detachment and novelistic powers of observation were not only inappropriate but also a sort of alibi. The plea of being elsewhere, at my blameless typewriter, when the crime was committed would not stand up any more for an American writer; opposition to the war was not a sufficient credential to permit me to circulate here as a pure recording sensibility noting down impressions, which, however, I was doing and could not help doing, short of jumping out of my skin. It came down to this: if I was an unsuspicious source, worthy of belief, so far as a wide American public was concerned, this meant I was a suspicious character to all who mistrusted that public's standards and morality—including myself. On the other hand, the command (if that is not too strong a word) of an audience was my value to the North Vietnamese, and if I vacated that little seat of judgment I had pre-empted years ago and resigned the duties, perhaps inflated by vanity, that went with it, then I might as well have stayed home.

Everybody knows that you cannot serve God and Mammon, but few can refrain from trying; they count on being the exception, especially if, as in my case, they do not set out to serve Mammon but allow Him, as they think, to serve *them*, since that seems to be His whim. For my generation, Stalinism, which had to be opposed, produced the so-called non-Communist Left, not a movement, not even a sect, but a preference, a political taste shared by an age group resembling a veterans' organization, which had last seen action during the Spanish Civil War. Since the "brand" of radicalism we preferred had no appeal for the masses (only the CIA, as it turned out, was interested), we had no clear alternative but to be "believing" socialists and practicing members of capitalist society. My own socialism consisted in voting for Norman Thomas until he vanished from the ballot and in anarchist and libertarian sympathies; there was a time in the forties when I might genuinely have tried to live in an anarchist utopia. The dream of a New Jerusalem, which would be my private Calvary (since I am not a willing crank), has stayed with me in reverie, merging more and more with the commonplace let's-get-away-from-it-all desert-island fantasies whose seat seems to be in the liver—the longing for a "cure." Hence my questions to Pham Van Dong about decentralization. Meanwhile, like most of the non-Communist Left, I was moving effortlessly into a higher and higher income bracket. The slight discomfort this caused me was outweighed by the freedom from any financial stringencies and the freedom to write exactly what I wished.

That freedom (cf. Norman Mailer) is a perquisite of successful U.S. authors. Until I came to Hanoi, I had joyed in the exercise of it as in the performance of some faintly dangerous athletic feat, which continues to surprise the doer each time it is brought off. There were not so many good things to point to in our country, and to be the embodiment, the living proof, of one of them is reassuring: "Watch me, young man, and learn how to do it. In our country, you do not have to sell out to sell." In Hanoi, for the first time in my travels, I found that this freedom and the material evidences of it, in the shape of clothes and possessions, were not regarded as enviable. The number of my suitcases (I have never learned to travel light) may have afforded some slight amusement; that was all. The license to criticize was just another capitalist luxury, a waste product of the system. This of course is true. The fact that you can read about, say, police brutality or industrial pollution in the New York *Times* or even in a local paper is nothing to be especially proud of, unless something concrete results, any more than the fact that you can read both sides about Vietnam and watch it on television. A free press is livelier than a government-controlled one, but access to information that does not lead to action may actually be unhealthy, like any persistent frustration, for a body politic. The illusion of being effective, the sole justification of my presence there, began to waver in North Vietnam the more I called upon it to defend me against the charge of complicity with American ruling circles—a complicity attested by the mirror. All the excess mental baggage I carried, of allusion and quotation, the "acquirements" of college, study, travel, acquaintance with prominent figures, weighed as heavy as my suitcases, as my unenvied freedom. My objectivity was making me uncomfortable, like a trade mark or shingle advertising a genuine Mary McCarthy product ("Trust Her to Speak Her Mind"). In short, I was not pleased with myself, or with what I somewhat showily represented.

But if I was nothing but a sample of American society—a feeling that grew on me—then I had no subjectivity at all. Yet I was aware of a subject, an "I," asserting itself from time to time, in protest or scruple, a subject I did not dislike. What I was carrying around with me, too, and not as an encumbrance, was a remnant of Christian ethics, applying to my own conduct and to the world at large. A vision of harmony and a universal pardon, with everybody being forgiven and getting married in the end, as at the finale of *The Marriage of Figaro* or a Shakespearean comedy. Whatever jarred or distressed me in North Vietnam—the history lesson on the blackboard in Hung Yen Province, the extirpation of French, the monothematic narrowness of art and literature—had to do with the loss of universals. The private tumults and crises I had been undergoing, trivial as was their occasion (who cared whether I wore that ring made from a shot-down plane or whether I said "puppet" or

127

"Viet Cong"?), involved the omnipresence, the ubiquity of God. *He* cared. Being an unbeliever made no difference. I had swallowed Him too many times as a child at the communion rail, so that He had come to live inside me like a cherry stone growing or like Socrates' unshakable companion and insistent interlocutor: oneself.

What remained from my Catholic training was the idea that it was necessary to be the same person at all times and places. When alone, I must never perform an action (short of taking a bath, etc.) that I would be unwilling to perform in public. This applied, of course, to thoughts, since God could hear you thinking them. It was the same choral vision of unity and concord, on a piping individual scale, that I still wished to see enacted in a free socialist commonwealth, though I had found it only in art, which is probably the only place where it is native. And it was because of such essentially God-fearing scruples that, as I got to know the North Vietnamese better, I grew ashamed to write little observations about them in my notebook, for you ought not to be two people, one downstairs, listening and nodding, and the other scribbling in your room.

The North Vietnamese, very likely, would have had no hesitation in drawing up a full report every evening on my companion and myself. But their ethic is in the service of the state, society, and mine is more selfish, mainly working at my own salvation. There lay the conflict of values, obscure because in practice the results may look similar, since both strive for correction of base or "low" tendencies. Here, however, more analysis is required. Since I have no trace of belief in a future life, what is meant by "my own salvation"? It comes down, I think, to a simple question of comfort. I am concerned with my own comfort, being able "to live with myself," as people used to say. And that, in a nutshell, was why I had come to North Vietnam.

Patriotism, I had surmised, had played a large part in my decision to go, and this was true, as far as it went. I could not bear to see my country disfigure itself so, when I might do something to stop it. It had surprised me to find that I cared enough about America to risk being hit by a U.S. bomb for its sake, having detested flag-waving from the days when we were made to "pledge allegiance" in school every morning. But if I *were* killed, I argued, it might at least convince a few Americans that civilian targets were being aimed at. I was not a military objective. On the other hand, other Americans over their fresh-frozen orange juice would be saying "It served her right."

Possibly yes, for I have come to recognize that I went chiefly for my own peace of mind. To put it as basely as I can, if my country stopped that brutal, brutish onslaught, I would be able once again to enjoy my normal pursuits. Reading, writing, spending money, looking at pictures and cathedrals, entertaining friends. Sleeping. Paying my income tax. I was still doing all those things, except sleeping, pretty much as formerly, but with a disturbed conscience, like a public-relations counsel pulling at my elbow, and hence without pleasure. If I could only make that hideous war go away, everything would be as before. That, of course, was a mistake. Nothing will be the same again, if only because of the awful self-recognitions, including this one, the war has enforced.

"*Vous avez beaucoup de coeur, madame,*" Pham Van Dong

said. He was talking about my little book on South Vietnam; someone had translated extracts into French for him. "You have shown a deep feeling for the Vietnamese people. Feeling and understanding. *Ça m'a touché*." Guiltily, I wondered (as many of my critics might) whether he did not mean someone else— perhaps Martha Gellhorn? Then it came to me that the parts he had read must have been about the lepers and the refugee camps. Later in the conversation he came back to the subject, as though I had made too little of it, brushed it aside too rapidly. I thanked him again. Would I write a book about the North, he wanted to know. It was too early to say, I replied. Perhaps only a couple of articles. It would depend on how much material I had. "I can't make a book out of something that isn't one." I feared he was disappointed by this stiffening of artistic integrity. "I would *like* it to be a book," I said.

Later I heard via the grapevine (Hanoi, as I say, is a small world) that the Prime Minister had been much impressed by my honesty in refusing to say that I would be writing a book when in fact I was in doubt about it. *"Oui, oui, il a parlé de cela."* My heart jumped with pleased surprise. This, then, was the universal pardon. I was set free. He had kissed us, each, with emotion when we said good-by, and now I did not have to feel like a Judas, whatever I would write. The North Vietnamese did not expect more of me than what I was. From each according to his abilities, which is the same as saying, in my Father's house, there are many mansions.

It would be pleasing if the story of my visit could stop there. . . . But it has an epilogue. In Phnom Penh, waiting for me at the airport, was the wife of the West German ambassador to Cambodia. On my way through, she had asked me to try to learn something about the fate of Dr. and Mrs. Krainick of the Medical School of Hue University, who had disappeared during the Têt offensive; the rumor had reached Bonn that they had been captured by the Viet Cong and were being held to treat their wounded. Knowing Dr. and Mrs. Krainick, I did not feel this would be too bad. They had treated all patients alike, and it was thanks to Mrs. Krainick in particular, who came to see me impulsively in my bedroom at the house of a U.S. official, that I had learned some of the truth about conditions in Hue. But in case they needed an advocate, I pleaded their cause at some length when we visited the NLF Delegation. As it turned out, this was not necessary. They knew about the Krainicks, had known about them long before the Têt offensive. Good people, yes, and "*plus ou moins sympathiques à nous.*" Mr. Tien, the Chief Delegate, had already been making inquiries, and they were not with any Viet Cong unit. According to his information, they had last been seen in the university compound. He feared they might be dead —killed in a bombing raid.

Nevertheless, I still had hope. In the steaming airport, I told the German ambassador's wife exactly what the Front leader had said. She stopped me, shaking her head. "We have just had news. They are dead. Their bodies have been identified." Later I read that the Krainicks and another German doctor had been found in a mass grave, executed by the Viet Cong. Or possibly, other sources suggested, by the North Vietnamese Army, who would not have known about them. Still another theory was that they might have been murdered by Buddhists; the Krainicks were Catholics, and during the Têt offensive, old

scores in Hue were settled—going back to the Struggle Movement of 1966—between Buddhists and Catholics. Certainly the
Krainicks had enemies among the town officials; last year the
story was that Dr. Krainick was not allowed to enter the hospital
laboratory because of his angry complaints about local corrup-
tion. There is no way of knowing yet what really happened, and
I feel somewhat suspicious of American stories of mass graves.
And if the Viet Cong summarily buried the Krainicks, does this
prove that it killed them? According to the news story from
Saigon, the other bodies found in the grave were those of Hue
notables—very likely some of their bitterest enemies. Such an
injustice is hard to bear, on the Krainicks' behalf, and worse is
to think that, after all, it *may* have been the Viet Cong who did
it; no army or guerrilla band fails to commit an occasional act
of senseless, stupid butchery. I should prefer to think it was the
Americans, indiscriminately bombing, which would not have
taken the doctor and his wife by surprise or wounded their feelings. After eight years of service in Hue, they must have been
used to seeing civilian victims of American bombs and being
told there was nothing *personal* about it. . . . With the Viet
Cong, it was different; the young Germans working with the
Krainicks had explained to me that they regularly drove the
Red Cross station wagon into VC territory, along roads the
Americans would not venture to take unless heavily armed, in
convoy, and preferably not even then. When I had applauded
their courage, they said it was only common sense: "They know
we help them when they are sick or wounded, so why should they
shoot at us?"

Assuming it was the Viet Cong—or, slightly less terrible, the

132

North Vietnamese—I cannot step forward with an excuse. No power has vested me with the authority to condone the murder of civilians. This came easy to a young militant of the New Left, who told me brusquely that people like the Krainicks had no business in Vietnam: they should either have joined the Viet Cong or gone back to Germany. That it was absurd to expect a middle-aged, middle-class German Catholic couple to do *more* than practice charity (a rare and difficult virtue) cut no ice with him. What happened to them was their own fault for trying to be disinterested do-gooders. *"Plus ou moins sympathiques"* was insufficient. Such people, he added, were obsolete.

If they were obsolete, what was the point of killing them? The ideas of that young man are far from the principle of limit governing the North Vietnamese conduct of the war and far from the "correctness" usually shown by the Viet Cong in their dealings with the civilian population. In fact, they are much closer to the views of the American command, which demands that the population take sides; anybody who remains in a hamlet designated Viet Cong is liable to execution from the air. Our position is that they got what was coming to them for sticking around.

The only excuse for the Krainicks' murder is that it happened and cannot be retraced now, whoever did it. Whoever did it has shouldered a crime that time may pardon or events may avenge. Eventually this war will become "ancient history," water over the dam. If time did not exercise that forgiving power, embodied in the principle of amnesty, nobody could live another second. The North Vietnamese, a mature people, as they say, know this, carefully distinguishing the person of the criminal from his crime, treating the fractures of the shot-down pilots with their advanced surgical skills (did Dr. Tung operate in such cases or did he leave it to his assistants?) and conducting them to air-raid shelters, separate but equal, when the sirens blow.

But Johnson and his advisers, perhaps because of the magnitude of their offenses, cannot even yet accept the ineluctable ending of the war and are literally fighting it off. Their maneuvers suggest that they are seeking the impossible: not the general forgetfulness accorded by time—who remembers the French cabinets of the years before Dien Bien Phu?—but exoneration. The hope of this fades, obviously, whenever peace nears. Might makes right is the only history lesson Johnson appears to have learned, and as he approached the brink of peace last April 3, he grew frightened. In the months that have passed, he has got over his scare. What forces can combine again to lead him to the edge and push him over into the pit, as he has assessed it, of destruction? The mere traction of opinion will not do it. Opinion, like Johnson, wavers, as is shown by the fact that no candidate for his office, however favorable to "peace," has been able to face meeting it under its other name, *surrender*. The moral overtones are displeasing to the American public; surrender is a confession of failure. Yet we will be lucky, though we do not see it, if failure, finally, is the only crime we are made to confess to.